AMERICAN EDUCATION

Its Men,

Ideas,

and

Institutions

Advisory Editor

Lawrence A. Cremin
Frederick A. P. Barnard Professor of Education
Teachers College, Columbia University

AMERICAN EDUCATION: *Its Men, Ideas, and Institutions*
presents selected works of thought and scholarship that have
long been out of print or otherwise unavailable. Inevitably, such
works will include particular ideas and doctrines that have been
outmoded or superseded by more recent research. Nevertheless,
all retain their place in the literature, having influenced educational thought and practice in their own time and having provided
the basis for subsequent scholarship.

THE KINDERGARTEN

IN AMERICAN EDUCATION

BY

NINA C. VANDEWALKER, B.L., M.Pd.

ARNO PRESS & THE NEW YORK TIMES
*New York * 1971*

Reprint Edition 1971 by Arno Press Inc.

Reprinted from a copy in
  The Newark Public Library

American Education:
  Its Men, Ideas, and Institutions - Series II
ISBN for complete set: 0-405-03600-0
See last pages of this volume for titles.

Manufactured in the United States of America

Library of Congress Cataloging in Publication Data

Vandewalker, Nina Catharine, 1857-1934.
    The kindergarten in American education.
    (American education: its men, ideas, and
institutions. Series II)
    1. Kindergartens--U. S. I. Title.
II. Series.
LB1205.V3 1971   372.21'8'0973   75-165732
ISBN 0-405-03721-X

THE KINDERGARTEN

IN AMERICAN EDUCATION

Mrs. Carl Schurz.
The first kindergartner in the United States.

THE KINDERGARTEN

IN AMERICAN EDUCATION

BY

NINA C. VANDEWALKER, B.L., M.Pd.

DIRECTOR OF KINDERGARTEN TRAINING DEPARTMENT, MILWAUKEE
STATE NORMAL SCHOOL. FORMERLY CRITIC TEACHER IN
MICHIGAN STATE NORMAL SCHOOL, AND TEACHER
OF METHODS IN WHITEWATER STATE
NORMAL SCHOOL

New York
THE MACMILLAN COMPANY
1908

Norwood Press
J. S. Cushing Co. — Berwick & Smith Co.
Norwood, Mass., U.S.A.

FOREWORD

WHEREVER the democratic idea has emerged during the past century it has been accompanied by certain movements which have tended to anchor and hold it fast. Of all such social phenomena the kindergarten has been one of the most interesting and enduring.

German thinkers had been for half a century consciously imaging the universal ideals of freedom and unity in their literature, philosophy, and art. "The Faust," "The Ode to Joy," "The Ninth Symphony," and Novalis' "Blue Flower" were embodiments of that national spirit which had been inarticulate for two centuries. At last the *Idee* craved political expression and midway down the century all Europe was stirred by spirited revolutions. These revealed the extent to which men's hearts were reanimated with courage and humanitarian purpose. New social programs were offered by patriots and freethinkers to the several governments under agitation. For the most part these were rejected or proscribed, and their authors cast out across the waters, only to propagate and quicken the democratic idea wherever they were received. The United States being made by and for such as these, they came from Germany, Hungary, Italy, Ireland, and Bohemia with the ideal of liberty more consciously enthroned in their minds than ever before.

In spite of the enforced exodus and immediate failures, a new ideal had been made to shine out before men, and they now centered their hope and faith upon schemes of reconstruction by means of child education and child preservation. It was then that the kindergarten was reached out for by the rational-minded, more or less well understanding its remedial nature. An inevitable welcome awaited it in our own country, where it has proved its basic worth, by moving naturally and steadily forward on the national stream, which is ever rising toward its level of a true democracy.

And now another half century has passed away, pressed down and running over with pioneer intensities and exigencies, and we look back and register the facts of this movement and call it history.

The story of the kindergarten in America involves the naming of great statesmen, public-spirited men and women, far-seeing philanthropists and noble thinkers, as well as a host of public and private educators who have faithfully, even heroically, served to project the idea into the practice of our public school system.

The pioneer stages are well over and the time has come for these records to be made accessible to all students and practitioners of education.

It is therefore with peculiar gratification that I welcome this history of the kindergarten in America, by Miss Nina C. Vandewalker, who is so eminently well prepared to be its historian. Miss Vandewalker has had unusually successful experience in grade and normal school teaching, in supervising both primary and kindergarten work, as well as in kindergarten training. To this practical equipment Miss Vandewalker has also added that of the serious scholar. Her able articles have appeared in our leading scientific journals, and her just and accurate accounting of both the past history and present tendencies in elementary education commands the respect and admiration of the entire teaching profession.

A history of the kindergarten in America cannot fail to widen and deepen the public understanding of this unique movement, to know which, " root and stem, and branch and all," involves a composite knowledge of philosophies as old as Socrates, psychologies as new as yesterday, and the whole range of habits, activities, sentiments, and tendencies native to human life.

AMALIE HOFER.

CHICAGO COMMONS, 1907.

PREFACE

THE kindergarten is an accomplished fact in American
life and education. That it embodies the fundamental
principles of child training, that it has become a part of
the school system in every progressive community, and
that its principles are being increasingly applied in elementary education are matters of common knowledge.
If one seeks, however, for definite information concerning
the origin, growth, or present status of the movement in
the United States, he is at a loss. Books treating of different phases of kindergarten theory or practice are numerous, it is true, and articles have been written describing the
origin and growth of the movement in different centers; but
the attempts thus far made to summarize the movement as
a whole have either been too brief to give its general scope,
or have been published in a form not readily obtainable.
This book is the outgrowth of a recognized need for a
survey of kindergarten progress in the United States.

The articles that have appeared in the kindergarten
periodicals from time to time describing the work in the
different cities have played an important part in advancing
the kindergarten cause, and the publication of the most
important of these in book form would make a valuable
contribution to educational literature. While such a

collection would furnish many facts of kindergarten history, it would fail, however, to give what is equally needed, — an insight into the movement as a whole, and into its relation to other movements that have shaped American life and education. The kindergarten movement, like other movements, must be seen in its proper perspective before it can be correctly estimated. To portray the kindergarten movement in its relation to American education as a whole is the difficult task which the author has attempted in this book. The treatment which this calls for must of necessity lack in concreteness, and therefore perhaps in interest, for the average reader at least, but it is hoped that the limitations which the form of treatment imposes may be compensated for by the added insight that will be given into the movement as a whole.

The author recognizes that it may not be the part of wisdom to discuss movements whose full significance has not yet been revealed, since conclusions now drawn, or interpretations now made, may be valueless in the near future. She feels, however, that there is need for a statement of the movements that have brought about the present differences in· theory and practice among kindergartners, although the time may not yet have come to estimate them correctly. She considers that the theory and practice of the kindergarten, as well as that of education as a whole, are being slowly evolved, and that no one school of thought alone will furnish it. Although an interpretation of current tendencies may have but a passing value, therefore, she maintains that some statement of these tendencies is needed to make present conditions intelligible, even though in the near future a restatement may be needed.

The information given in the following pages has been obtained from many sources. Among these are: Barnard's *American Journal of Education;* the Reports of the Commissioner of Education and of the National Educational Association; the bound volumes of *The Kindergarten Magazine* and *The Kindergarten Review;* and Miss Anderson's *Kindergarten Annual.* The histories of education in the United States by Boone, Dexter, and Butler, as well as Monroe's " Text-book in the History of Education " and Martin's " The Evolution of the Massachusetts School System " have been freely consulted, as have many other books and periodicals quoted in the text. Talcott Williams' article on " The Kindergarten Movement," published in *The Century;* Susan E. Blow's " History of the Kindergarten in the United States," in *The Outlook;* and Hamilton W. Mabie's article on "The Kindergarten in America," also published in *The Outlook,* have likewise proved valuable and suggestive.

Much information has also been obtained from correspondence. That concerning legislation authorizing the establishment of kindergartens in the different states of the Union has been obtained largely from the Superintendents of Public Instruction in the different states. The information concerning the kindergarten in temperance, welfare, and missionary work has also been obtained largely from correspondence. The author takes this occasion to thank all those who have rendered such assistance.

She wishes to acknowledge her special indebtedness to the late Carl Schurz and to his daughter, Miss Agatha Schurz, for information concerning the life of Mrs. Schurz, and for permission to use her picture; to Mr. Charles H. Doerflinger of Milwaukee for the loan of a complete file of *The New Education;* to Mr. C. W. Bardeen, of Syracuse, N.Y., for the loan of two volumes of *The Kindergarten Messenger* and other books now out of print; and to Mr. Manfred J. Holmes, Secretary of the National Society for the Scientific Study of Education, for permission to use portions of the article on " The History of Kindergarten Influence in Elementary Education," which appeared in the Sixth Year Book of that society. She wishes to express her thanks to Miss Anna Webster Lytle of the Milwaukee State Normal School; to Dr. Edward L. Thorndike and Dr. John A. MacVannel of Teachers College; and to Miss Amalie Hofer of the Pestalozzi-Froebel Training School of Chicago for valuable suggestions and for reading the completed manuscript.

NINA C. VANDEWALKER.

MILWAUKEE STATE NORMAL SCHOOL,
MILWAUKEE, WIS., *December,* 1907.

CONTENTS

CHAPTER   PAGE

I. THE KINDERGARTEN IN RELATION TO EDUCATIONAL
PROGRESS 1

II. THE PERIOD OF INTRODUCTION; KINDERGARTEN
BEGINNINGS 12

III. EARLY LITERATURE 25

IV. THE PERIOD OF EXTENSION; GENERAL CHARAC-
TERISTICS 37

V. KINDERGARTEN ASSOCIATIONS AND WOMEN'S CLUBS 55

VI. THE KINDERGARTEN IN CHURCH, SUNDAY SCHOOL,
AND MISSION WORK 76

VII. THE KINDERGARTEN IN TEMPERANCE, SETTLEMENT,
AND WELFARE WORK 103

VIII. THE KINDERGARTEN AND EDUCATIONAL ORGANIZA-
TIONS AND EXHIBITIONS 129

IX. PROGRESS IN KINDERGARTEN LITERATURE . . 159

X. THE KINDERGARTEN IN THE PUBLIC SCHOOL
SYSTEM 183

XI. KINDERGARTEN INFLUENCE IN ELEMENTARY EDU-
CATION 209

XII. NEW TENDENCIES 232

APPENDIX 257

INDEX 269

THE KINDERGARTEN IN AMERICAN EDUCATION

CHAPTER I

THE KINDERGARTEN IN RELATION TO EDUCATIONAL PROGRESS

THE kindergarten movement is one of the most significant movements in American education. In the fifty or more years that have passed since the first kindergarten was opened in the United States education has been transformed, and the kindergarten has been one of the agencies in the transformation. Although it came to this country when the educational ideal was still in the process of transformation, its aims and methods differed too radically from the prevailing ones to meet with immediate acceptance. The kindergarten is, however, the educational expression of the principles upon which American institutions are based, and as such it could not but live and grow upon American soil, if not in the school system, then out of it. Trusting to its inherent truth to win recognition and influence, it started on its educational mission as an independent institution, the embodiment of a new educational ideal. Its exponents proclaimed a new gospel — that of man as a creative being, and education

B   I

as a process of self-expression. They substituted activity for the prevailing repression, and insisted upon the child's right to himself and to happiness during the educational process. They emphasized the importance of early childhood, and made the ideal mother the standard for the teacher. They recognized the value of beauty as a factor in education, and by means of music, plants, and pictures in the kindergarten they revealed the barrenness of the old-time schoolroom. By their sympathetic interpretation of childhood, their exaltation of motherhood, their enthusiasm for humanity, and their intense moral earnestness they carried conviction to the educational world. The kindergarten so won its way to the hearts of the people that the school at last opened its doors and bade it welcome. It has become the symbol of the new education.

The acceptance of the kindergarten in the United States has not depended wholly upon the attitude of the school, nor upon the recognition of its pedagogical value. The kindergarten was the outgrowth of the idealistic philosophy which so profoundly influenced the world's thought during the century just closed. As the influence of that thought made itself felt in American life, the thought of the people became receptive to the kindergarten message. Until the conception of man as spiritual had been emphasized in the American pulpit, the church and Sunday-school would not have been ready for Froebel's suggestions concerning the child's spiritual development. Until the mission of art to humanity had been recognized, the emphasis which the kindergarten places upon beauty as a factor in education would not have been understood. Until the heart of America had been stirred to a new sense of human brotherhood, the significance of the kindergarten as an agency for the salvation of neglected childhood would not have been appreciated. Until the school conceived of education as something more fundamental than instruction in the Three R's, the doctrine of education by development would not have been selected as the foundation for educational procedure. The progress of the kindergarten cannot be fully understood, therefore, without a glance at the history of American thought during the latter part of the nineteenth century. Its progress in relation to elementary education cannot be adequately comprehended without an acquaintance with certain significant facts in American school history during the past fifty years.

The building up of the American school system has been a slow process, — one not yet satisfactorily completed. It began, not at the bottom, with the work of the youngest children, but at the top. In fact, the value of early childhood for educational purposes was the last to be recognized and the work of the youngest children was the last to be provided for. The primary school had to win its way into the school system much as the kindergarten is now winning a place there. For many years children were not allowed to attend the "reading and writing schools" until they were seven years of age, and even then only on the condition that they had already learned to read.   Even after primary schools were established they were not regarded as a part of the school system; both in and out of New England — in Boston until 1854 — they were managed independently. It was not until about 1860 that the present system of grading was established.   A complete revolution in educational thought was therefore necessary before the kindergarten could hope for recognition.   Had Froebel himself come to the United States, as he at one time thought of doing, his message would have fallen upon deaf ears, for until the importance of early childhood for educational purposes began to be recognized, the kindergarten could have no meaning.   It is not strange, therefore, that the ten kindergartens opened in the United States before 1870 — with one exception established by educated Germans — should have attracted relatively little attention.

Before the kindergarten could hope for general recognition, however, other important changes in educational thought were necessary.   While education was looked upon as a process of instruction in the Three R's only, the kindergarten could hope for little or no recognition. When that conception gave way to one of development, the fundamental value of kindergarten theory and practice became apparent.   Although the older view has not been entirely supplanted even yet, it was practically unquestioned until after the organization of the graded school system — until the Civil War.   The growth of the psychological conception of education which in the United States began to make itself felt at about this time, was a gradual one toward which many influences and individuals contributed. Probably no one person's influence did more in the early years than that of Dr. E. A. Sheldon, the founder of the Oswego Normal School. Dr. Sheldon had come under the influence of Pestalozzi's principles and methods while superintendent of schools in Oswego, N.Y., and in 1861 he opened in the city schools a department for the training of teachers on Pestalozzian principles. That there is a natural order in the child's development and that this order must determine the character of early education was the principle especially emphasized. This called for objective teaching and self-expression in the early years, however, not primarily for instruction in the language arts. The work based upon these principles proved so successful that in 1863 the little training class in the city schools was organized into a state normal school. The success and enthusiasm of the graduates of the Oswego Normal School was such that they were sought for in nearly every state in the Union. With the gradual acceptance of the new views the kindergarten began to assume significance, and its message no longer fell on unheeding ears.

The insight into the psychological conception of education brought about by its successful application at Oswego was doubtless one of the causes for another advance in elementary education having an important bearing upon kindergarten progress. This was the addition of drawing and manual training to the elementary curriculum. The introduction of these subjects indicated

a new trend in education, — a trend in the direction of
activity as a principle in school work. This principle
is basic in the procedure of the kindergarten, but until
the value of activity for the pupils in the grades began to
make itself felt the message of the kindergarten was but
partially comprehended. But the adoption of this principle — the first outward indication of which was the
introduction of drawing into the schools of Boston in
1870 — had not come without effort, and was the result
of practical considerations rather than of pedagogical
insight. The necessity for art instruction as a factor in
education had been impressed upon England by the
London Exhibition of 1851, and the awakening of England
had had its effect upon American education. The value
of art education had been further emphasized by the Paris
Exposition of 1867, and the introduction of drawing into
the schools of Boston was the result. The advocates of art
teaching realized, however, that the value and feasibility
of such teaching needed demonstrating to the people at
large. The opportunity for such a demonstration was
furnished by the Philadelphia Exposition of 1876. The
exhibit of drawing and manual training work made by
the Boston schools on that occasion was the direct stimulus
to the introduction of these subjects into the schools of
the country. Competent authorities have declared the
addition of these two subjects, drawing and manual training, to be "the most notable educational advance of the
past two decades." "Throughout all the long hundred
years in which they had been building a nation, Americans

had shown themselves children of utility, not of beauty,"
says Woodrow Wilson. "Everything they used showed
only the plain unstudied lines of practical serviceability.
The things to be seen at Philadelphia, gathered from all
the world, awakened them to a new sense of form and
beauty. Men knew afterward that that had been the
dawn of an artistic renaissance in America, which was
to put her architects and artists alongside the modern
masters of beauty, and redeem the life of the people from
its ugly severity."

The recognition awarded at the Philadelphia Exposition
to the lines of work upon which the kindergarten had from
the beginning placed the greatest stress, brought that
institution a recognition not accorded it before, and
another step was taken in the preparation for its general
acceptance. The friends of the kindergarten were not
satisfied, however, with a recognition of its principles alone.
They felt that the institution as such had a mission in
American life and education, and had, seen in the Exposition the opportunity for presenting its message to the
American people. A model kindergarten on the Exposition grounds had been arranged for, which was carried
on for the entire time that the Exposition was in progress.
The message it had to offer was heard and understood,
and from that time on its acceptance was assured.

For the two decades following the Philadelphia Exposition the main lines of educational advance were the
introduction of courses in drawing and manual training
into the schools of the country, and the incorporation of the

kindergarten into the school system. The kindergarten did not always yield the results for grade work that its friends anticipated, however, since the aims of the kindergarten and those of the school lacked unity of purpose. The attempted application of kindergarten principles to the higher grades was frequently disappointing for the same reason. The new studies too — drawing, manual training, and nature study — were often merely additions to the curriculum, without an insight into their real purpose and value or their relation to the traditional studies. For this, and other reasons too complex for discussion here, the need of a more fundamental educational theory began to be felt. The response to this need was the "new psychology " — the psychology of James, Hall, and others — which began to make itself felt during the last decade of the century. The new psychology, of which the child study movement was the natural outgrowth, had a most important bearing upon kindergarten progress. The nature of its bearing upon that progress must be reserved for a later chapter. Suffice it to say in passing, however, that the new psychology set the seal of its approval upon the main features of kindergarten procedure and upon the application of its principles to grade work. To many it gave their first insight into the aims and purposes of the kindergarten; to others it reinterpreted the Froebelian doctrines and gave them a broader significance. The new psychology therefore prepared the way for an appreciation of the kindergarten and of the other movements in education that would have been impossible before.

An acquaintance with the general progress of American thought thus briefly outlined will serve as a background against which the progress of the kindergarten may be seen in clear relief. A new conception of education was necessary before the significance of the kindergarten could be comprehended, but this alone would not have accorded it the place it now holds in popular esteem. A new Christianity too was needed, no less than a new ethics, and a new insight into the mission of art. The "new theology " no less than the "new psychology" has played a part in advancing kindergarten progress. The social reformer doubtless proclaimed the message of Froebel as effectively as did the educational expert. Visions of a new theology, a new ethics, a new art, and a new education began to dawn upon the American people during the years immediately following the Civil War. The struggle for the realization of the new ideals characterized the last two decades of the century. From the standpoint of kindergarten progress the first of these periods — from the opening of the first kindergarten in 1855 until after the Philadelphia Exposition — may appropriately be called the Period of Introduction; the second the Period of Extension. The first period divides itself naturally into the period of the German kindergarten, — from 1855 to about 1870, — and the period from 1870 to 1880 or thereabouts when the kindergarten was accepted by Americans as an institution adapted to American conditions and American needs. The period of extension falls likewise into two subdivisions. During the first of these — from

1880 to 1890 — the kindergarten was accepted with relatively little question; during the second — from 1890 until the present time — a more critical attitude has set in, and a reconstruction of its theory and practice is demanded. The dates given are general and approximate only, as the movement has differed radically in its origin and progress in different localities. There are many sections of the country where the period of introduction is still to be entered upon; there are others where the kindergarten is known and theoretically appreciated, but where its extension into the school system has not yet been effected; there are others still — not infrequently kindergarten strongholds — where no evidence appears that the criticisms made upon its procedure during the past ten years have been heard or heeded. These differences are not surprising. Where the movement has been primarily philanthropic, where it has come into no contact with progressive school work and educational leaders, it is not surprising that the older views should obtain. Where the work brings the kindergartner into a constant association with those of larger outlook, it would be little to her credit if the newer views did not prevail. The periods outlined are intended to serve as a framework against which the progress of the kindergarten may be seen in its relation to the progress of elementary education as a whole.

It is too early for a complete history of the kindergarten movement, but the general demand for information upon the subject, more comprehensive and available than the

magazine articles or summaries in the Report of the Commissioner of Education, which have heretofore been the
main sources of knowledge, has led to this brief statement
of the main facts of kindergarten history. It is intended
primarily for the younger kindergartners, to whom an
acquaintance with the movement with which they are
allied is essential to intelligent effort. It aims also to
acquaint the younger school men of the country with one
of the vitalizing influences in American education during
the past quarter century, and to lead them to a study of
the Froebelian philosophy. If it succeeds in showing
them the reasons for the differences that prevail among
kindergartners at the present time, and in securing their
coöperation in the problem of adjusting the kindergarten
to the school, it will have rendered a needed service.

CHAPTER II

The Period of Introduction; Kindergarten Beginnings

THE first kindergarten in the United States is popularly supposed to have been the one opened in Boston in 1860 by Miss Elizabeth Peabody, but the real beginning of the movement must be placed several years earlier and ascribed to a different source. The European Revolution of 1848 brought to the United States many Germans of culture and influence, who during the decade between 1850 and 1860 established private schools, bilingual in character, in all the larger cities in which their countrymen had settled, — New York City, Hoboken, Detroit, Milwaukee, Louisville, and several others. It was in these schools, based upon the principles of the new education, which at that time had found little or no recognition in the United States, that the kindergarten in the United States had its real origin. Although these schools did not attract from American educators the attention which their excellence deserved, and hardly a mention can be found of the kindergartens that most of them contained, their indirect influence in behalf of the new education in general and of the kindergarten in particular was considerable. The whole kindergarten movement in Wisconsin can be traced to the efforts made in its behalf by those in charge of the German-English Academy of Milwaukee, — an institution of the kind in question, and this is not an isolated instance. The German-English Academy at Louisville, Ky., and that at Detroit, Mich., as well as the institution in Newark, N.J., of which Dr. Adolph Douai was principal, did effective service in promoting the spread of the new institution. Although several of the earliest kindergartens were private and independent, the impulse that led to their organization came from the same general source. With the single exception of Miss Peabody's, the ten kindergartens established in the United States before 1870 all owed their origin to the movement in question. The first kindergarten in the United States was one in the home of Mrs. Carl Schurz, in Watertown, Wis., in 1855. The second was that opened by Miss Caroline Louise Frankenburg in Columbus, Ohio, in 1858. As far as can be learned, the first of the German-English institutions to adopt the kindergarten was Dr. Douai's school, to which reference has already been made. The kindergarten became a part of that institution in 1861. A kindergarten was opened in Hoboken, N.J., at about the same time, and three years later two were opened in New York City. One was opened in West Newton, Mass., in 1864 by Mrs. Louise Pollock. The inspiration of the kindergarten ideal came to Dr. William N. Hailman in 1860, during a visit to the schools of Zurich, Switzerland, and in 1865 he added a kindergarten to the German-English Academy of Louisville, Ky., of which he was president. It was in this kindergarten that Mrs. Eudora L. Hailman found the inspiration to her life work, and that she and her husband began their thirty years of united service to the kindergarten cause. The German-English Academy of Detroit adopted the kindergarten in 1869, and in 1873 organized effort in its behalf was undertaken by the German-English Academy of Milwaukee. There is little record of the effort made by these institutions or by the private kindergartens thus established to influence existing educational procedure, but the indications are that such influence was much more widespread than has been supposed.

The efforts made in behalf of the kindergarten by Dr. Henry Barnard and Miss Elizabeth Peabody are fairly familiar to the educational public, but the relation between these efforts and those of the German exponents of the kindergarten has never been adequately shown. Dr. Barnard visited England in 1854 as a delegate to the International Exhibit of Educational Systems and Materials, and while there became deeply interested in the kindergarten. English interest in the doctrines of Froebel had been awakened in 1854 by the lectures of the Baroness von Marenholz-Buelow, Froebel's foremost disciple, and by the practical work of Madam Bertha Ronge, who had been a pupil of Froebel and an active worker in the kindergarten cause in her native city of Hamburg. With Madam Ronge had been associated her sister, Miss Margaretha Meyer, also a pupil of Froebel. Dr. Barnard made a report of the educational exhibition in general and of the kindergarten in particular to the governor of Connecticut

upon his return. He also described the exhibit of kindergarten materials in an article in the *American Journal
of Education*, of which he was the editor. The report in
question and the article, published in 1856, were, as far
as known, the first articles concerning the kindergarten
to appear in print in the United States. Between the
time of Dr. Barnard's London visit and the publication of
the articles, however, the kindergarten itself had appeared
upon American soil. Miss Meyer had become the wife
of Carl Schurz, and had come to the United States, settling
in Watertown, Wis. In order to give her own children
the advantages of kindergarten training she gathered
together the children of relatives who lived near, and
taught them the kindergarten songs, games, and occupations in true Froebelian fashion. This was, as has been
stated, the first kindergarten in the United States.

Dr. Barnard's report concerning the kindergarten had
awakened the interest of Miss Elizabeth Palmer Peabody,
who is usually considered the apostle of the kindergarten movement in the United States. The interest thus
awakened was deepened by an article which appeared in
the *Christian Examiner* in 1859. This article, written
by Mrs. Edna D. Cheney and Miss Anna Q. T. Parsons,
was a description of the kindergartens of Germany and a
summary of Froebel's principles as stated by the Baroness
von Buelow. Miss Peabody at once undertook the study
of Froebel, and a chance meeting with Mrs. Schurz during
a visit of the latter to Boston in the winter of 1859 fanned
her interest into a flame of enthusiasm. Having gained

from Mrs. Schurz an insight into the practical details of conducting a kindergarten, she opened the kindergarten associated with her name the following year. "Miss Peabody had participated in the great social, literary, religious, and philosophical movement somewhat vaguely described as New England Transcendentalism," says Miss Blow, "and was peculiarly fitted both by natural endowment and experience to enter into the thought of Froebel." She was at this time fifty-five years of age, and in the full maturity of her powers. As sister-in-law of Horace Mann she had come into vital contact with the great educational movement identified with his name. She was a close friend of Bronson Alcott, in whose unique educational experiment she had shared. She had taught for years also in another private school of considerable note. That she gradually realized from the inadequacy of her results that the philosophy of Froebel needed a deeper study than she had given it; that she went to Europe in 1867 for the additional study which she considered necessary; and that she devoted the remaining years of her active life to the advancement of the kindergarten cause by teaching, writing, and lecturing, are facts well known to the student of educational history.

The significance for elementary education of the decade from 1870–1880 has already been commented upon. It was a significant decade for the kindergarten movement also, not alone because influences favorable to the kindergarten were set into operation at that time, but for other reasons as well. One of the indications of advance in the kindergarten movement was the establishment of kindergarten training schools, the first of which was opened in Boston in 1868 by Madame Matilde Kriege and her daughter. These ladies were pupils of the Baroness von Marenholz-Buelow, who had been induced to come to Boston by Miss Peabody. In 1872, Miss Henrietta B. Haines, the principal of a large private school in New York City, invited Miss Maria Boelte to open a kindergarten in her school. Miss Boelte was a pupil of Froebel's widow, who had achieved marked success both in England and in Germany. Her work in New York attracted much favorable attention. At the close of the year Miss Boelte married Professor John Kraus, already an exponent of the kindergarten, and together they established a kindergarten training school which is still in existence, although it has been carried on by Madame Kraus-Boelte alone since Professor Kraus's death in 1896. As trained kindergartners were thus becoming available, kindergartens multiplied rapidly. The kindergarten found a foothold in Washington, D.C., in 1870 through the efforts of Mrs. Susan Pollock, and its influence was strengthened in 1872 by the establishment of a training school under Miss Emma Marwedel. In 1873 several German kindergartens were established in Milwaukee, through the agency of the German-English Academy of that city, and when the following year Professor W. N. Hailman succeeded to the presidency of that institution, kindergarten training was instituted also. The year 1873 saw the beginning of the kindergarten training movement in St.

c

Louis, under the leadership of Miss Susan E. Blow, and the following year saw the beginnings of the movement in Chicago, under the leadership of Mrs. Alice H. Putnam. In 1875 kindergartens were opened in Indianapolis and in Los Angeles, Cal., and in 1876 in Denver and San Francisco, as a result of a lecturing tour by Dr. Felix Adler, who espoused the kindergarten cause almost from the beginning. The Philadelphia Exposition acquainted the Quaker City with the new institution, and when the Exposition closed, Miss Ruth Burritt, the "Centennial kindergartner," remained in Philadelphia to open a kindergarten and a kindergarten training school. The kindergarten spread rapidly during the latter part of the decade, the result in part of the larger acquaintance with it for which the Philadelphia Exposition had furnished the opportunity. The friends of the kindergarten had recognized the opportunity which the Exposition would afford, and had planned accordingly. The Exposition kindergarten was conducted in an annex to the Woman's Pavilion, by Miss Ruth Burritt of Wisconsin, who had had several years of experience as a primary teacher before she became a kindergartner, and whose manner and insight were such as to gain adherents for the new cause. The enclosure for visitors was always crowded, many of the on-lookers being "hewers of wood and drawers of water, who were attracted by the sweet singing and were spellbound by the lovely spectacle." Thousands thronged to see the new educational departure, and many remained hours afterwards to ask questions. The Exposition marked

an epoch in the advancement of the kindergarten movement, as it marked an epoch in the history of elementary
education.

The ready acceptance of the kindergarten after the
Philadelphia Exposition did not imply a recognition of its
pedagogical value alone; in fact it is worthy of note that
many of the kindergartens established at this period were
philanthropic in their ultimate purpose. As the rapid
growth of cities and the increasing immigration was fast
developing the slum with its attendant evils, people were
beginning to realize that some antidote must be found.
The value of the kindergarten as a child-saving agency
was at once recognized, and churches and philanthropic
societies took up the movement. The first charity kindergarten was opened in 1870 in the village of College Point,
N.Y.; others were opened the same year in Cleveland,
Ohio, and Florence, Mass. In speaking of this phase
of kindergarten work in the Report of the Commissioner
of Education, Miss Laura Fisher says:—

"Centering among, and concerning itself with, the
children of the poor, and having for its aim the elevation
of the home, it was natural that the kindergarten as a
philanthropic movement should win great and early
favor. The mere fact that the children of the slums were
kept off the streets, and that they were made clean and
happy by kind and motherly young women; that the
child thus being cared for enabled the mother to go about
her work in or outside the home — all this appealed to the
heart of America, and America gave freely to make these

kindergartens possible. Churches established kindergartens, individuals endowed kindergartens, and associations were organized for the spread and support of kindergartens in nearly every large city."

The fact that kindergartens could be carried on successfully under public school conditions was satisfactorily demonstrated by the experiment made in St. Louis, Mo., by Superintendent William T. Harris and Miss Susan E. Blow. But for this experiment the general introduction of the kindergarten into the schools of the country — accomplished in large part during the following period — might have been postponed for many years. Dr. Harris was at this time acknowledged as the leading exponent of the idealistic philosophy in the United States, and as such he had actively espoused the kindergarten cause. Miss Blow was a native of St. Louis who had taken a course of kindergarten training in Miss Boelte's school. Superintendent Harris had recommended the adoption of the kindergarten as a part of the school system to the St. Louis school board in 1870, but the first step in that direction was taken in 1873, when Miss Blow offered to superintend a kindergarten and instruct a teacher gratuitously, if the board would provide the teacher, the room, and suitable equipment. The offer was accepted, and the kindergarten was so successful that additional ones were soon called for. A training school was organized, as Miss Blow preferred to train her own co-workers, and new kindergartens were opened as fast as kindergartners could be trained. The success of the experiment made

St. Louis the center of interest among school men, and educators from all parts of the country coming to visit, the stimulus was carried to their respective cities. Dr. Harris severed his connection with the St. Louis schools in 1880 and Miss Blow withdrew from the work that she had so successfully inaugurated in 1884, but by that time the practical value of the kindergarten as a part of the school system had been demonstrated to the satisfaction of the educational public.

The friends of the kindergarten movement in Wisconsin looked even farther than the introduction of the kindergarten into the public schools. They wished to secure its adoption by the normal school system of the state, and to provide for the training of kindergartners at state expense. Because of the many German residents of the state who had brought an acquaintance with the kindergarten from the land of their birth, the movement in Wisconsin had made considerable headway before it came into contact with the movement as it had developed in other sections of the country. In 1870 a vigorous campaign had been undertaken in Milwaukee which had resulted in 1873 in the organization of kindergartens in the four German-English institutions of that city. Professor William N. Hailman's acceptance of the presidency of one of these institutions in 1874 had not only strengthened the kindergarten sentiment among the German-speaking people, but had also brought it to the attention of the English-speaking people of the city and state. The first English kindergarten in Milwaukee was organized by Mrs. Hailman, and training classes were undertaken in both languages. A campaign for the introduction of the kindergarten into the schools of Milwaukee and into the normal school system of the state was undertaken. The second of these objects was accomplished during the decade under consideration, and the first soon after the opening of the following one. A kindergarten was opened in the State Normal School at Oshkosh in the spring of 1880, — "the first kindergarten officially and directly connected with any state normal school in the United States." A similar movement had been undertaken in Minnesota, and a few months later a kindergarten department was also opened in the State Normal School of Winona.

The organization of the National Educational Association in 1872 had afforded another means of stimulating interest in the kindergarten on the part of school men. At the first meeting Professor Hailman, then of Louisville, Ky., had presented a paper on "The Adaptation of Froebel's System of Education to American Institutions," and urged the appointment of a committee to examine the system. The committee, consisting of Professor John Kraus, John Hancock, Dr. Adolph Douai, William T. Harris, George A. Baker, J. W. Dickinson, and William N. Hailman, made a most favorable report the following year, and the impression made by the report was strengthened by a paper read before the Association by Mrs. Kraus-Boelte. In the years immediately following, the cause of the kindergarten was kept before the Association by Mrs. Kraus-Boelte, Dr. Harris, and Professor Hailman.

At the end of the decade the friends of the kindergarten had abundant reasons to rejoice at the progress of the cause. In 1870 there were less than a dozen kindergartens in existence, all save one established by Germans and conducted in the German language; in 1880 there were not less than four hundred scattered over thirty states. In 1870 there was one kindergarten training school in the United States; in 1880 such schools had been established in the ten largest cities of the country and in many smaller ones. The year 1870 saw the establishment of the first charity kindergarten; in 1880 the new institution had become recognized as the most valuable of child-saving agencies, and mission kindergarten work had become so popular among wealthy young women as to be almost a fad. The practicability of the kindergarten as a part of the school system had been successfully demonstrated, and the logical sequence of its future relation to the school had been recognized by the establishment of kindergarten training departments in the normal school systems of two great states. The National Educational Association had set the seal of its approval upon the principles which the kindergarten embodied, and had commended the institution to the school men of the country for experiment and consideration. "The lessons of the Philadelphia Exposition, at which the meaning of the art and industrial elements in education was first revealed to the American teachers," had been taken to heart, and the result of the awakening it had occasioned had been the attempted enrichment of the elementary curriculum by the addition of the subjects frequently termed "fads," — music, drawing, manual training, nature study, and physical culture. The fact that these subjects constituted an organic part of the kindergarten awakened an interest in that institution on the part of many who had thus far given it but little attention. They began to see in the kindergarten games the true beginning for the child's physical development; in its gift and occupation exercises the foundation for art and manual training work; and in its garden work and nature excursions the foundation for a true knowledge of nature. The significance of the kindergarten as the logical foundation for a new system of education had therefore begun to dawn, and the comprehensiveness of the Froebelian philosophy stood out in striking contrast to the meagerness of the educational theory which then prevailed. The period of its apprenticeship was therefore over. Its advocates could silence doubt and criticism by pointing to results already achieved, and could urge its extension with the faith and enthusiasm born of the assurance that it met a recognized need in American life and education.

CHAPTER III

The Period of Introduction; Early Literature

THE present familiarity with the spirit and method of the new education makes it difficult to comprehend the curiosity with which the first kindergartens were regarded and the difficulty that people experienced in understanding its philosophy. Even a slight acquaintance with the views generally held a generation ago will show that the difference between the views of life of the twentieth century and those of the period of the Civil War is world-wide. The idealistic philosophy, of which the kindergarten is the expression, considers the universe fundamentally spiritual, and nature and humanity as but varying expressions of the World-Spirit, — God. Man is therefore in essence good, and education is a natural process of unfolding his spiritual capacities, in accordance with the universal laws of evolution. This doctrine has permeated every phase of the world's thinking during the past quarter century, and no longer seems strange and unfamiliar; but at the time in question there had been little to familiarize the American people with such views. It is not surprising, therefore, that the kindergarten which embodied them should have appealed most strongly to the highly educated and the spiritually minded in the early days, and that its American sponsors should have been the New England Transcendentalists, — the American exponents of German idealism. The acceptance of the idealistic interpretation of the universe, reinforced later by the doctrine of evolution, then hardly yet formulated, and the new interpretation of Christianity in terms of social value, — these have given to the life and education of the present generation a depth and a significance that it lacked a generation ago.

The few, therefore, caught the real significance of the new institution in the early years; the many saw, and comprehended but in part. Education in a guise so different from that which she had hitherto worn was practically unrecognizable. Visitors came, — too many for the well-being of the children or the comfort of the kindergartner; but, aflame with the enthusiasm of a new insight, she bade them welcome, hoping to gain new converts to her educational faith. The kindergartner of to-day, beginning work in a new locality, encounters few of these difficulties. She deepens the interest of the inquiring or silences the doubts of the skeptics by referring them to Froebel or his many interpreters, or by pointing to the results the kindergarten has accomplished in other localities. The kindergartner of the early day had no such resources. She must be, perforce, the priestess of the new cult, for available literature there was practically none. Froebel and his European exponents were hidden from the majority in the fastnesses of a foreign language. It is not surprising, therefore, that the translation of kindergarten literature should have been thought imperative, and that the spread of that literature should have been considered an essential part of the movement. Had not the philosophy of Froebel contained fundamental truth it could never have kindled the enthusiasm needed to overcome the almost unsurmountable obstacles. The literature of the kindergarten, containing as it does the new philosophy of education in a nutshell, has been a significant factor in shaping educational ideals, and no study of the movement can be considered complete that does not include a résumé of its development.

The beginnings were insignificant enough. The brief mention of the kindergarten in the *Journal of Education* in 1856 and 1858, and the admirable exposition that had appeared in the *Christian Examiner* in 1859, had, as has been stated, acquainted a few people with the existence of the new institution. Charles Dickens, the first great English student of the kindergarten, had written for *Household Words* in 1855 an article on "Infant Gardens," as kindergartens were called when first introduced into England. This article was written for the purpose of calling attention to the work of the Baroness von Marenholz-Buelow, who had come to England the year before to introduce the kindergarten system. "This article must always take a front rank as a strikingly clear, comprehensive, and sympathetic exposition of the principles and processes of the kindergarten," says Professor James L. Hughes. The Baroness herself had written a pamphlet on "Infant Gardens" also, and her co-workers, Madam

Ronge and her husband, had written a "Practical Guide to the English Kindergartens." These articles had received considerable attention in the United States.

In 1862 an article in the *Atlantic Monthly* by Miss Peabody, entitled "What is a Kindergarten?" attracted further attention to the movement, and the interest awakened by the article and the kindergarten itself led Miss Peabody to the publication of her "Kindergarten Guide" the following year. This consisted of two parts, — an exposition of the kindergarten by Miss Peabody, and a treatise on "The Moral Culture of Infancy" by her sister, Mrs. Horace Mann, who had herself been a teacher and a co-laborer with her husband in his efforts for the advancement of education. About four thousand copies of the "Guide" were sold. The following year Mrs. Louise Pollock of West Newton, Mass., already mentioned, translated one of the German kindergarten manuals. She also wrote a series of articles concerning the kindergarten for a magazine called *The Friend of Progress.*

To familiarize the public still further with the kindergarten and with the educational principles that it represents, Miss Peabody wrote for the New York *Herald*, in 1867–1868, a series of articles upon the subject. The following year Miss Peabody, Mrs. Mann, the Baroness von Buelow, and others wrote a series of articles on the kindergarten and child culture in general for *The Herald of Health.* The editor of this magazine was Dr. M. L. Holbrook, "the first journalistic friend of the kindergarten." He had been connected with Dr. Dio Lewis in his efforts for the advancement of physical culture, and was at that time connected with the Hygienic Institute of New York City, which advocated the cure of the sick by hygiene and right living — a new idea at the time.   These articles did much to acquaint a progressive class of people with methods of child rearing more rational then those which had thus far prevailed.

Among the leading contributors to the advancement of the kindergarten idea at this time was Professor John Kraus, a friend of Froebel, who had settled in San Antonio, Texas, in 1851.   Professor Kraus had contributed to American journals frequent articles upon the Froebel-Pestalozzian methods, a series in *The Army and Navy Gazette* having attracted considerable attention.   Recognizing the value of his acquaintance with the educational thought of Germany, Dr. Barnard had invited him in 1867 to become a member of the staff of the Bureau of Education.   During the year he had contributed to the Washington papers a valuable series of articles upon the nature and purposes of the kindergarten.   In 1870 and 1871 he translated a pamphlet by the Baroness von Buelow, and made an elaborate report upon the kindergarten for the Report of the Commissioner of Education.   In this and other ways he helped to keep the kindergarten cause before the public.

To acquaint the public with the value of the new system of child training was one of the purposes of the friends of the movement during the early years, but another need speedily developed.   As the demand for kindergartners increased and adequate opportunities for kindergarten

training were still lacking, many with little or no preparation attempted to open kindergartens. It soon became
evident that if these were to continue, technical instruction
in the use of the kindergarten instrumentalities was needed.
It was to meet this need that Mrs. Pollock had translated
one of the German manuals in 1865, and that Edward
Wiebe had prepared his "Paradise of Childhood" in
1869. It was because Professor Kraus and Mrs. Kraus-
Boelte felt that these books did not sufficiently indicate
the use of the materials and meet the needs of the many
partially trained kindergartners that they undertook later
what is undoubtedly their most important contribution to
the movement, the "Kindergarten Guide," the first
installment of which appeared in 1877.

During the decade between 1870 and 1880 several important books were written and translated. The first
of these in order of time was "The Kindergarten; A Manual for the Introduction of Froebel's System of Primary
Education into the Public Schools," by Dr. Adolph
Douai of Newark, N.J., the principal of one of the first
German-English institutions in the United States to adopt
the kindergarten.   In 1872, Madam Matilde Kriege
made a free translation of the Baroness von Buelow's
"The Child," and in 1873 Professor William N. Hailman
wrote his "Kindergarten Culture."   The lectures by which
the Baroness von Buelow had converted Paris to the
kindergarten cause were translated in 1876 under the title
"Education by Labor," and her "Reminiscences of
Froebel" was translated by Mrs. Mann the following year.

Madam Kraus-Boelte's "Guide" also appeared during 1877. Several of Miss Peabody's lectures had appeared from time to time in pamphlet form. Through the translations of Miss Josephine Jarvis and Miss Fanny Dwight in 1879, Froebel's "Mother Play and Nursery Songs" was made accessible to English readers. The same year Dr. Holbrook translated and published "From Cradle to School" by Bertha Meyer, and Mrs. Pollock a collection of "Kindergarten Songs and Games." All these helped to satisfy the increasing demand for a fuller knowledge of the kindergarten, and the philosophy of which it is the embodiment.

An important step in the advancement of the kindergarten was taken in 1873, when Miss Peabody established *The Kindergarten Messenger*, a monthly magazine of twenty-four octavo pages. This was especially needed at this time, as it acquainted the scattered workers with each other, and afforded a means of communication between them. In addition to reports from leading workers, correspondence, and general educational intelligence, it contained original articles, theoretical and practical, by leading kindergartners. The translation of "Reminiscences of Froebel," "Education by Labor," and other books appeared first in its pages. It gives a vivid picture of kindergarten conditions during this introductory period, and the personality of the gifted editor is felt in every page. It is a veritable mine of data for the future historian of the movement.

The fortunes of the little magazine were varied. In the

Peabody number of *The Kindergarten Review*, Miss Emilie Poulsson says: "Miss Peabody had her struggle in maintaining the *Messenger*. The list of subscribers was never long, and not all of these were so good as to pay their dues. The editor records that one year it covered its own expenses, but that did not happen twice. Although all her own service was given free there was much financial worry connected with the enterprise, and she was often grateful for the kind help received from one or another of her friends." The *Messenger* continued through 1873, 1874, and 1875, but the next year it became a department of *The New England Journal of Education*. This arrangement, however, did not satisfy Miss Peabody, and in January, 1877, she again took the magazine into her own hands and ran it to the end of the year. As the thousand subscribers needed to meet expenses could not be obtained, it was merged in *The New Education* conducted by Professor Hailman, then of Milwaukee.

The kindergarten interest that Professor Hailman had found existing in Milwaukee, and the financial support offered by Mr. Carl H. Doerflinger of that city, had enabled him to establish in 1876 the periodical in which *The Kindergarten Messenger* had now been merged. *The New Education* was an eight-page magazine, issued monthly. In the first number Professor Hailman thus stated the purpose of the new publication. "Froebel and Herbert Spencer are the principal exponents of the new education; the kindergarten, Froebel's great gift to man, is the first decisive practical step toward a realization of its require-

ments. To aid in the propagation of the views of Froebel
and Spencer on education; to render the former, particularly, better known; to contribute in spreading the bless-
ings of kindergarten culture in its genuine form and to
make war upon all efforts for establishing spurious systems
under cover of the honored name, — are the purposes of
The New Education." Like *The Kindergarten Messenger*
it contained practical articles for mothers and kindergartners, news concerning the spread of the new educational
gospel, translations from standard German educators, discussions of current educational questions, and vigorous
and incisive editorials. Its scope was broader than that
of its predecessor, and it played a most important part in
advancing the kindergarten cause and in shaping the
educational policy of the Northwest during its formative
period. Professor Hailman modestly ascribed much of
the credit to the unwearying generosity of the publisher,
Mr. Doerflinger, who for years sent the periodical free to
the leading school men of the state. He says: "We have
little doubt that to this generosity, aided by his personal
effort as a member of the State Board of Normal Regents,
Wisconsin is largely indebted for her present advanced
position on the questions discussed in *The New Education.*"
After six years of existence it went the way of its predecessor, and was merged in *The Public School* of Boston.
Like its predecessor it is invaluable for the educational
historian.

The record of the kindergarten literature of the period
would be incomplete without reference to the annual school

D

reports of the superintendents in those cities which had adopted the kindergarten. Dr. Richard G. Boone considers that "the reports of school officers and educators include by far the largest part of America's contribution to the literature of education." He says: "But the most complete and systematic presentation of educational philosophy is to be found in the annual reports of Superintendent William T. Harris, while superintendent of the St. Louis schools, from 1867 to 1880." Three of these dealt with the kindergarten. That of 1875–1876 discussed its philosophy; that of the following year the results of the kindergarten in the St. Louis schools, and that of 1878–1879 the history of the St. Louis kindergarten system. Although these reports seldom reached the general public, they were read by the leading school men of the country, and did much to shape educational opinion. The same is true of the articles on the kindergarten read before the National Educational Association, and embodied in the reports of that organization.

No statement concerning kindergarten progress in the United States during this period would be complete without a reference to the two principal kindergarten supply and publishing companies, the Milton Bradley Company, of Springfield, Mass., and the Steiger Company, of New York City. Mr. Bradley's life experience had prepared him for conversion to the kindergarten cause in 1869, and through the improvement he has made in kindergarten material and the assistance rendered in the publication of kindergarten literature, he has won deserved recognition among kindergarten workers. Mr. Steiger, too, rendered valuable assistance during the early years. His confession of kindergarten faith was made in the publisher's preface to Madam Kriege's translation of "The Child." He says: "The publisher of this book is resolved to expend his best energies in the interest of education. He has witnessed with lively satisfaction the progress of education in this country; but while appreciating the good that has been done, he agrees with the opinion of many that the system is capable of improvement. He has, therefore, embraced the cause of the kindergarten, as best calculated in his judgment to inaugurate a thorough educational reform; and he will gladly entertain proposals for the publication of other works on the subject and cheerfully coöperate with school authorities, associations, and individuals whose aim is the amelioration of existing modes of instruction."

If the friends of the kindergarten had reason to rejoice at the progress of the institution itself during the decade under consideration, they had no less reason for satisfaction at the increase in its literature. In 1870, there were in the English language, as far as known, but four books on the kindergarten, — Madam Ronge's "Practical Guide to the English Kindergarten," Miss Peabody's "Kindergarten Guide," Mrs. Pollock's translation of a German manual, and Wiebe's "Paradise of Childhood," a compilation from several such manuals. During the decade five important books had been translated in the United States, — the Baroness von Buelow's "The Child,"

"Education by Labor," and "Reminiscences of Froebel"; Froebel's "Mother Play and Nursery Songs," and Bertha Meyer's "From the Cradle to the School." Four books had been written, — Douai's "The Kindergarten," Hailman's "Kindergarten Culture," Madam Kraus-Boelte's "Guide," and Mrs. Pollock's "Kindergarten Songs." In addition to this, hundreds of articles had appeared in newspapers and magazines, and several pamphlets had been printed, — some for free distribution. *The Kindergarten Messenger* and *The New Education* had scattered the new ideas still farther. The seed-sowing was surely plentiful. The harvest will be traced in succeeding chapters.

CHAPTER IV

The Period of Extension; General Characteristics

THE recognition that the kindergarten had thus far obtained had made its extension a mere matter of time, but the history of its progress since 1880 has been inextricably interwoven with the history of American life and thought as a whole, and with that of elementary education in particular. Until that time the progress of the movement had been measured mainly by the increasing number of kindergartens opened; while such increase continued during the period in question, it constituted but one phase of kindergarten progress. The great advance made during the period was the general incorporation of the kindergarten into the school system, and the application of its principles to elementary education. This was not accomplished in a day or even in a decade. Even the quarter century that had passed since the date mentioned has not brought about the general adoption of the kindergarten as an institution or the general application of its principles to primary education. If the new movements which the Philadelphia Exposition had suggested could, with the dawn of the new decade, have been introduced into every city in the land by royal edict or magic power; if fully equipped kindergartens and complete drawing and manual training courses could have been put into operation everywhere by the pressing of a magic button at the stroke of an imperial clock, it would doubtless have retarded instead of advanced the ultimate progress of the kindergarten, the school and the American people.   Insight into the new tendencies could not but be superficial at first, and the deepening of insight was a need that required time before the many-sided significance of the new movements could be grasped. This has been proved by the experience of more than one city in organizing its art and manual training courses, for example, upon a practical rather than upon a psychological basis.   Some of these found themselves upon the wrong track after a time, and adopted a new course. Some are on the wrong track still, and have never discovered it.   What has proved true of drawing and manual training has proved equally true of kindergartens prematurely introduced.   Some of these that have deteriorated into a mechanical routine may be seen even now.   This is also true of the so-called "kindergarten methods in primary work."   This was too often a superficial manipulation of kindergarten material with older children, without adequate insight into the principles that underlie kindergarten procedure.   Premature adoption and formulation have been the cause of many a failure, not in education alone.   The apparent lagging of the footsteps of progress was therefore in many respects a blessing in disguise.

The remedy was time, and the influences that were at

work among the American people deepening their intellectual and spiritual life in spite of other influences that were
tending to its deterioration. "Few quarter centuries in
the world's life bristle with salient events as does that
following 1870," says E. Benjamin Andrews in discussing
the political significance of the period. An estimate of
its significance in the history of American thought would
accord it a like commendation. There was a new stir
in the pulses of the nation when the more immediate and
vexing problems resulting from the Civil War were dis-
posed of. The great development of the nation's industrial resources was increasing its wealth, and this increase
in turn was developing the intellectual and spiritual
power of the people. In response to the increasing demand for higher education, a veritable renaissance set in.
Colleges multiplied alike for men and women. Graduate
departments came into existence to meet the need for
advanced and specialized instruction. New sciences
opened up attractive vistas and promises of almost un-
limited power. The new psychology and the newly
organized social sciences led into absorbing fields of thought
hitherto practically unknown. New ideals had dawned
upon the colleges themselves and the passion for social
service was born.

But this was merely one phase of the general enrichment of life. There had been art and artists during the
earlier part of the century, as the names of Copley, West,
and Stuart testify, but art had never been an organic part
of the national life. "The Puritan immigrants of New

England had all the abhorrence of art which had marked the followers of the Reformation, and for two centuries the bare, whitewashed walls of their plain meeting-houses were eloquent in protest against the art adornment of ancient church or chapel," says Isaac Clarke in "Education in the United States." "Nor did the long, hard struggle to wrest sustenance from stony soil or stormy sea afford any space of leisure for those artistic occupations that to the stern Puritan were worse than folly," he says further. As a result, however, of indirect causes too complex for analysis here, and the immediate stimulus of the Philadelphia Exposition, an immediate wave of art enthusiasm spread over the country, which during the past quarter century has been steadily increasing. In 1870 there were but ten institutions in the country that gave any form of art instruction, but four art museums, and a complete poverty of art treasures of any kind. In 1880 the number of art schools had increased to over thirty, and there had been a corresponding increase in the number of museums and galleries. Before the century closed one hundred seventeen art schools and forty-one art galleries had been established. Some of the schools and galleries have an international reputation.

The demand for art knowledge and instruction that had brought about such results had been fostered in part by the schools themselves, in part by art exhibitions and lectures, and in part by the first-hand acquaintance with the world's great masterpieces, gained by the increasing army of tourists to the historic galleries of Europe. It was strengthened by the growing number of American students who sought abroad the opportunities that their own country did not yet afford, and who upon their return taught in new forms the great ministry of beauty to the life of humanity. This sudden awakening of thousands to the significance of the world's art treasures can only be compared to that other period in the world's life when a young and virile people came into unexpected possession of the priceless heritage of Greek and Roman thought. Samuel Isham says in the "History of American Painting": "Taking a whole nation whose ideals, although high, had hitherto been purely material, intellectual, and moral, and endowing it with a perception of the beauties of art is an accomplishment without any parallel — at least on so large a scale." That the art appreciation of the people as a whole is still undeveloped must be admitted, but the value of art as a stimulus to the higher spiritual life will never again be questioned.

Along with the awakening to the value of pictorial and decorative art came a like awakening in the world of music. The value of music as a factor in elementary education had been recognized for a generation before pictorial art had been accorded such recognition, and there had been a gradual growth in musical taste and feeling instead of a sudden awakening to its significance. There had been much seed-sowing in the musical field during the generation that had passed since Lowell Mason had secured the introduction of music into the public schools of Boston in 1838, and the harvest surpassed in richness the hopes of even the most sanguine. "There are few periods in the history of any country in which the progress of art has been so rapid as the progress of music since the Civil War," says Mathews in the "History of American Music." The war had been a great awakener of mind and it had stirred the emotional life of the people to its very depths. This gave a power of interpretation that comes only from profound spiritual experiences. Before this time the centers of musical life and interest had been in the East — in New York and Boston chiefly. The interest now spread to all parts of the country, and it was not long before Cincinnati and Chicago rivaled their sister cities in musical appreciation and in the opportunities offered for musical study. Musical societies were organized everywhere, and the musical masterpieces of the world, like the great masterpieces of painting and sculpture, came to have a significance for thousands to whom they had hitherto been but names. It was at this time that the conservatories and colleges of music now to be found in every large city, were founded and began to vie with the art schools in interest and prophecy of a fuller development for the youth of the land. "In these musical ambition and talent found opportunity for improvement, and for the acquisition of knowledge of the higher walks of art," says Mr. Mathews again. Residence and study in the musical centers of Europe on the part of many added to the insight gained, and raised the general standard of musical intelligence among the people at large. Since the themes of the great masterpieces deal with the fundamental experiences of human life or portray vital facts of Christianity, this growth of art insight could not but deepen and enrich the emotional and spiritual life of the people.   In the growing insight into and appreciation of the æsthetic, the foundations for a more fundamental education were being laid.

While the life of the people was thus gaining in emotional power along the æsthetic lines, it was taking on added richness in another direction, having apparently little relation either to art or to education, but in reality having the most profound significance for both.   The ethical and religious life of the people was undergoing a gradual change, — one that to many seemed an undermining of the very foundations of the social order, but that to others meant the reëstablishing of faith and virtue upon a deeper and firmer foundation.   Ever since civil authority had supplanted ecclesiastical authority in the control of education, fears had been expressed for the moral safety of American life.   A half century or more of nonsectarian education had, however, shown no such falling off in public morals as might have been expected if morality were dependent upon instruction in religious dogma.   But while such instruction is no guarantee of character there must be a foundation of spiritual life, both in the individual and in the nation — a recognition of the moral law and an obedience to it.   That the religion of creeds and observances is on the wane — among Protestants at least — none will deny; that there has been a compensating gain is becoming increasingly evident to all who are in touch with ethical and religious thought and the application of that thought to social conditions and problems. This gain has come in large part from the gradual reconstruction of religious thought necessitated by the doctrine of evolution. A new order of thinking and new motives to conduct could not but result from the acceptance of the view that man, as the highest expression of the omnipresent and eternal energy manifested in the universe, is ideally akin to that energy — God, and "if not made, at least making in the divine image;" that the moral law is the law of man's highest nature, and that the existence of such a law is evidence of a moral order in which humanity is grounded; that sin had its origin in the animal inheritance from which man is gradually emerging; and that redemption is the perfect and final emergence from the animal into the spiritual state. Such an interpretation of the fundamental doctrines of Christianity carried with it social implications that are far reaching in their consequences. It gave a new dignity to humanity, and brought with it a new sense of human brotherhood. It created a clearer vision of the kingdom of God on earth, and carried with it the conviction that the coming of that kingdom depended upon the agencies that society could put into operation, and could be hastened in no small degree. It brought with it a new and deepened sense of social obligation and a broader recognition of human rights. It resulted in the extension of social interest that is expressed in the social settlement and kindred institutions. Combined with influences from other sources it set the currents of present-day thought in the direction of social betterment and thus created the "social movement."

It is the new insight into the social significance of Christ's teaching that has brought the church face to face with new and intricate problems. To the question whether the church could, if she would, undertake the whole problem of man's salvation — material as well as spiritual — to which the interpretation in question seems to point, the institutional church is the provisional answer. Rev. Josiah Strong says in a recent article on the institutional church in *Current Literature:* "Many fail to perceive the profound importance of the religious changes which are taking place or to suspect that they are destined to produce a new type of civilization. For many years the church laid emphasis on man's relation to God, and forgot to emphasize his relation to man. The new emphasis laid upon the social teachings of Jesus is bringing a new order of civilization." The present problems of the church are therefore twofold: She must interpret her fundamental principles upon a new basis; and she must reorganize and enlarge her forms of activity. The passing from the old to the new ideals and forms of effort is no easy process, but the end toward which present thought is tending is becoming increasingly clear and results cannot but follow.

It is in part because the program of social reform that present conditions demand could not be undertaken by any church or federation of churches; and in part because of the growth of social interest and responsibility among the people at large, that philanthropic work, public and private, has assumed increasing importance and aroused increasing interest during the past few years. Charity had always existed and agencies for the relief of suffering in some of its many forms had been organized from time to time. But the increasing need for philanthropic effort which is due to a multiplicity of causes tending to the deterioration of life in the large cities, could not but challenge the thoughtful to a study of the conditions and spur to more serious effort the increasing enthusiasm for social reform. A study of conditions so complex called, however, for training of the highest order, and the rendering of efficient social service required a preparation not to be acquired by ordinary courses or methods. The growing recognition of these facts resulted in the establishment of departments of sociology in all the larger universities, and in gradually adding courses in social economics. This movement, combined with that successfully carried out in all the larger cities, — the organization of all relief agencies, secular and religious, into a Charity Organization Society, — will ultimately create a system of social betterment commensurate with the importance of the task. As the social and industrial life becomes more integrated, the improvement in material conditions is so interwoven with the development of higher ideals and the enrichment of the spiritual life that the two cannot be effectively provided for except through the coöperated effort that such an organization implies. Tenement and sanitary reform, improvement in the conditions of labor, protection from communicable diseases, the care of the destitute sick —

these and other forms of effort for social betterment are not only good in themselves, but also serve as important means of strengthening the moral and spiritual nature. The agencies that would relieve the spiritual poverty that causes in part the material ills; that would substitute thrift, sobriety, and virtue for incompetence, intemperance, and vice — do not they contribute materially to the betterment of the life that now is? Philanthropy so organized will become what it should be, — one of the great forces for the world's salvation.

It would be little to the credit of the social economist and his practical co-worker if the futility of work merely curative had not been forced upon him, and if the importance of preventive measures had not been recognized. That the cure of evil is indirectly preventive must be admitted, and much of the work mentioned has been and will be preventive in the large sense. But preventive work must be positive and direct as well as indirect. Such work must always be educational in character, and must begin with the children, the true subjects of education. It is not strange therefore that philanthropic interest should have centered in childhood and in the agencies for its salvation. The story of the efforts by which the rights of childhood — neglected, dependent, and delinquent — have come to be recognized is too long for recital here, and the list of charities, public and private, undertaken in its behalf too long to enumerate. The founding of societies for the prevention of cruelty to children — a check upon the ill temper of parents, the passage of laws preventing child labor, and the adoption of the probation system for juvenile offenders are of special significance. Childhood has other needs, however, than these,—the need for activity, inspiration, joy. These, too, modern philanthropy is increasingly providing. The city boy is no longer obliged to live in the streets; public playgrounds are being conceded as his right. He is not driven to crime from sheer ennui; library doors swing open, and settlement clubs and classes invite him to interesting forms of activity. Vacation schools, recreation piers, and fresh-air excursions furnish him with new experiences and give him an insight into the great world in which he must soon take an active part. The provision for such needs, pitifully inadequate as it still is, forms one of the most interesting chapters in the story of "the battle with the slum." Agencies for the relief of other kinds of need might have been organized at other periods in the world's history; those for furnishing childish happiness could only have been devised in recent years. It is significant that all these movements in the direction of constructive and preventive philanthropy had their origin in this country or were adopted from other countries during the years between 1870 and 1890. To-gether they contribute an influence for the upbuilding and ennobling of character that cannot but produce gratifying results in the near future.

The relation of the movements that have characterized American life during the past twenty-five years to elementary education in general and to the progress of the kindergarten in particular can be readily traced. The

new spirit in the universities and the consequent enrichment of the spiritual life of the people was loosening the
hold of traditionalism and strengthening the new conception of education. The new sciences in the universities and new methods in history and literature revealed
the emptiness of the elementary curriculum, based upon
the disciplinary conception of education alone, and the
need of "content studies" in the grades. The "new
psychology" and the introduction of courses in education
into the university curriculum not only gave a more fundamental insight into the nature of the educational process,
but it dignified education and placed it upon a scientific
basis. These new insights gave an added significance
to the kindergarten which embodies the views that were
coming into the educational consciousness. Up to this
time educational effort had centered itself mainly with
the problems incident to the period of organization. From
1880 on it began to occupy itself fundamentally with the
problems of educational theory. The last two decades of
the century became periods of reform and transformation.

The general development of artistic taste and musical
intelligence was tending also toward educational reform.
It seconded the dissatisfaction with the curriculum of
the Three R's where such a curriculum still prevailed;
it encouraged the introduction of the æsthetic element
into education; and it showed an appreciative interest
in the true purpose of the new studies where these had
already been introduced. As the kindergarten had
emphasized the value of beauty in developing the ideal

E

side of a child's life and had insisted upon plants and pictures in the kindergarten when there were none as yet in the school, its doctrines found particular favor, and an era of decorating schoolrooms and beautifying school grounds set in. The kindergarten therefore rose in favor and its doctrines aroused a new interest.

But the awakening of the public to the value of beauty as a factor in the child's development was not the greatest service that the kindergarten rendered to art education. The disciples of Froebel had urged their fundamental doctrine of creative activity, but the school had been slow to understand, and slower still to accept a doctrine so at variance with its traditional form of procedure. When artists, however, not only recognized the correctness of the principle but insisted that all art instruction should be based upon it, the public began to wake up. Verily, the stone that the educational builders rejected has become the head of the corner in the educational structure. It is in this particular respect that the kindergarten has been a positive influence in the transformation of the school.

The advancing musical intelligence likewise made itself felt in elementary education. The early musical work in the public schools had been confined almost wholly to teaching the musical notation. It was now seen that this was not the true foundation for a musical education, that music must be given a meaning to the child, and that a love of song must be developed before instruction in musical notation could have any significance. In other words, it was recognized that music, like representative art, must begin in feeling and intelligence, and not in technique. Although the music of the kindergarten left much to be desired in the early days of the movement, it was sufficiently different from that of the school to attract the attention of musical people and to indicate that it was based upon different principles. They recognized in the child's song, taught by rote, a means of cultivating his love of music, and in the various piano exercises a means of cultivating his musical intelligence and power of interpretation. For this reason also the kindergarten rose in public esteem. The musical teaching of the school has been reconstructed within recent years, and the kindergarten has been the determining element in that reconstruction.

Although the new views in religion and ethics and the new interest focused upon child saving have influenced school work and school methods less directly than have the more fundamental study of educational theory and the appreciation of the value of the æsthetic, the indirect influence of these new views has already been far-reaching. The opponents of the public school system have frequently pointed out the danger to American life from an education without religion. But as the new conceptions prevail, they will increasingly pervade educational thought and literature, and interpret the educational process as a spiritual one. When education has been so conceived, every study in the curriculum will contribute to the development of the higher life and the Power that makes for righteousness will be increasingly felt in and through the whole educational process. When teachers are inspired by such an insight, the absence of dogmatic instruction will not even be felt, for the purpose of education — the development of character — will have been attained. When this view of education — essentially the Froebelian view — was first presented, it seemed visionary and impracticable to all but the illumined few; the Froebelian emphasis upon the divinity of human nature seemed little short of sacrilege to those who had been accustomed to the doctrine of innate depravity only. Current interpretations of Christianity are quite in accord with the views which the kindergarten presents, however, and the kindergarten student not infrequently hears the doctrine presented in the class room reënforced from the pulpit. The larger acceptance of these views has given added weight to the philosophy of Froebel and to the kindergarten as its embodiment. Here, too, the kindergarten has been a positive influence. In the stimulus it has given to the progress of liberal views and to the study of the idealistic philosophy of which it is the outcome, it has not only paid a debt to philosophy and religion, but it has also been a means of enriching the life and thought of the country of its adoption.

The "social movement" with its interest in the agencies for child saving has had a more direct bearing upon the methods of the school than have the newer interpretations of religious doctrine. That a child's school work is affected by the character of his home and environment every teacher knows. That teachers have any moral responsibility for the lives of their pupils outside of schoolroom walls and schoolroom hours, that they have any responsibility for the social regeneration of the neighborhood in which their work lies, should such regenerating be needed, many of them, principals and superintendents included, would practically deny. It is not so specified in the bond of the school rules. It is just this responsibility that the forces organized for the betterment of childhood are trying to bring home to the conscience of the school. That the school has advanced by leaps and bounds during the past quarter century is readily granted. That its organization is on the whole good; that its curriculum possesses an interest it did not possess during the earlier period; and that its spirit and methods are constantly improving, none will deny. Its weakness lies in its failure to recognize its social and moral obligation to the neighborhood of which it is a part. Its aim is still largely intellectual and its duties too largely the duties of the schoolroom only. That social settlement clubs and classes, summer camps, vacation schools, and other similar agencies, frequently reach and quicken the lives of children with whom the school has failed is a matter of frequent comment. With due recognition of the difficulties of philanthropic effort arising from the limitation of the teacher's time and strength, the question may still be asked whether the passion for human betterment that has made itself so noticeably felt in the life of the people at large during the past two decades has permeated the school to the extent that it should. That something has come of the public agitation and interest is evident. The changes in the curriculum — the introduction of sewing, cooking, and manual training in general — are in part a response to this spirit. School authorities have aided in securing child labor legislation and in enforcing its application. They have coöperated with probation officers in eliminating juvenile crime, and with municipal authorities for the establishment of public parks and playgrounds. They have given active support to school decoration and outdoor art societies in beautifying schoolrooms and grounds, and in some instances have assisted in organizing school children's lunch stations. They have coöperated with social settlements and women's clubs in carrying on vacation schools and in many instances have eventually assumed their support. But the cry of the children is still heard. Here too the kindergarten has been a positive influence. In creating a new attitude toward childhood; in coöperating with the home to secure the best conditions for the child's development; in active efforts for the establishment of playgrounds, vacation schools, and similar agencies for children of all ages, the kindergartners of the country have contributed in no small degree to the cultivation of the philanthropic spirit in the teaching ranks. A more complete discussion of the service the kindergarten has rendered to education in this respect is reserved for the following chapters.

CHAPTER V

THE PERIOD OF EXTENSION; KINDERGARTEN ASSOCIATIONS AND WOMEN'S CLUBS

THE kindergarten in the early eighties was still in its experimental stage; it had demonstrated its value, but as yet to the few only. Before its general acceptance by the school system could be expected, an important work still needed to be done in its behalf. The movement needed to be illustrated on a large scale in strategic localities, and the value of the kindergarten as a child-saving agency demonstrated. To meet this need a new agency came into existence in all the larger cities, and in many of the smaller ones — the kindergarten association. Now that kindergartens have become general and departments for kindergarten training have been established in many state normal schools and other educational institutions, the important part that kindergarten associations have played in furthering the kindergarten movement is in danger of being lost sight of. The history of kindergarten progress would neither be intelligible nor complete, however, without a record of the service that such associations have rendered, not to the kindergarten alone but to education in general. They have differed in aim and scope, in the degree of influence exerted, in the method of procedure, and in the results accomplished, but their service in awakening educational thought and stimulating educational progress has been of inestimable value in American life. Some of these associations considered their work done when the kindergarten was incorporated into the school system. This was the case in Philadelphia, where thirty kindergartens were turned over to the city authorities by the Sub-Primary School Society, after six years of effort. Some associations affiliated themselves with the school authorities of their locality when these were ready to adopt the kindergarten, and coöperated with them in kindergarten maintenance and supervision, considering the cause best served in this manner. This plan has been successfully carried out by the Pittsburg and Allegheny Kindergarten Association. Still others organized to undertake a work supplementary to that of the school, whether or not the kindergarten was included in the school system. Such was the purpose for which the two associations in San Francisco were formed. Many of the associations formed in the early eighties are still in existence, although as a result of changed conditions their work has changed materially.

Kindergarten associations had been organized in a few cities before 1880, but the decade between 1880 and 1890 may appropriately be called the Association Decade in kindergarten history. Such associations had been organized in Milwaukee in 1870, and the establishment of kindergartens in the three German-English academies of that city was the result of their effort. As far as can be learned, California was the next to organize associations for the advancement of the kindergarten cause. The San Francisco Public Kindergarten Society was formed in 1878, and the Golden Gate Kindergarten Association of the same city two years later. The Cincinnati Kindergarten Association was organized in 1879, and the Froebel Association and the Free Kindergarten Association of Chicago in 1880. From that date on kindergarten associations were organized in the larger cities of the country, as nearly as can be learned, in the following order: The Sub-Primary School Society of Philadelphia in 1881; the Des Moines Kindergarten Association in 1882; the Indianapolis Free Kindergarten and Children's Aid Society, the Milwaukee Mission Kindergarten Association and the Kindergarten Association of Portland, Oregon, in 1884; the Los Angeles Kindergarten Association in 1885; the Kindergarten Association of St. Paul, Minn., of Providence, R.I., and of Cleveland, Ohio, in 1886; the Free Kindergarten Association of Louisville, Ky., in 1887; the Kindergarten Association of Albany, N.Y., and of New Orleans, La., in 1888; the New York Kindergarten Association, the Detroit Day Nursery and Kindergarten Association, the Denver, Col., Kindergarten Association, and the Kindergarten Association of Asheville, N.C., in 1889; the Kindergarten Association of Grand Rapids, Mich., and that of Chattanooga, Tenn., in 1890; the Kindergarten Association of Buffalo, N.Y., and of Minneapolis, Minn., in 1891; the Kindergarten Association of Galveston, Texas, of Charleston, S.C., and the

Pittsburg and Allegheny Associations in 1892; the Isabel Crow Kindergarten Association of St. Louis, Mo., the Kindergarten Association of Spokane, Wash., and the Columbian Kindergarten Association of Washington, D.C., in 1893. As the movement progressed other cities too numerous to mention organized similar associations. In 1897 the Commissioner of Education gave a list of over four hundred, and stated that a very large number of others had failed to respond to the request for information.

In spite of the differences in plan and purpose already referred to, the general aims of the kindergarten associations, wherever located, were much the same. These were at least threefold: to furnish helpful suggestions to young mothers in meeting the problems that their own children presented; to establish kindergartens and thus to advance the kindergarten cause; and to carry out a philanthropy that was increasingly felt to be necessary. These purposes were more or less interwoven. The study of childhood from the standpoint of Froebel's philosophy could not but lead to a higher appreciation of the kindergarten, and a desire for its extension and the establishment of kindergartens in needy districts was the most effective method at that time devised to carry out the desired philanthropy. The work of a kindergarten association, therefore, appealed to different classes of people and satisfied several different interests. Its work was shaped by these interests, though one phase or the other usually predominated.

Among the lines of work carried on, the mothers' classes must be given the first place. The serious discussion of the fundamental problems of motherhood and childhood from the viewpoint of Froebel opened up a new world of thought to many. It gave a new meaning to life and led to the formation of higher ideals and nobler purposes. The inspiration that the kindergarten association gave to thousands of young mothers was one of the reasons for its success. But this was not all. From the impulse first given by kindergarten associations to the study of childhood and the training for motherhood have come movements of national importance. The growing interest in the problems of child training led to the holding of a Mothers' Conference in Chicago in 1894, lasting for several days, under the auspices of the Chicago Kindergarten College. This proved so valuable that several similar conferences have been held since. The National Congress of Mothers, which held its first meeting in Washington, D.C., in 1897, was the indirect outgrowth of the interest thus aroused. Work of this character, whether national or local, could not but lead to a study of educational problems from other viewpoints than that of the home. It brought parents and teachers together for the discussion of mutual problems and enlarged the views of each. The results of this movement and the women's club movement of more recent years have given to American women an insight into educational problems that has done much to further the interests of education in the school.

The deepening insight into the problems of childhood

to which the mothers' study classes gave rise during the early years of the kindergarten movement was the foundation for the enthusiasm with which the second purpose of the kindergarten association — the establishment of kindergartens — was carried on.   The whole kindergarten movement in Chicago has grown out of a class formed by Mrs. Alice H. Putnam in 1874 for the study of Froebel. The class grew into a kindergarten association whose two hundred members were "all intelligent students of the kindergarten philosophy and practice."   An acquaintance with the practical working of a "mission kindergarten" would not fail to give these early students a new insight into the meaning of the kindergarten as an institution and lead them to place a higher estimate upon its principles. It could not but stimulate an interest in the kindergarten as such, its success elsewhere and its ultimate adoption by the school.   It invited comparison between the methods of the kindergarten and those of the school, and thus gave an added impetus to the influences that were already tending toward its transformation.

The acquaintance with the work of mission kindergartens for which the kindergarten association gave the opportunity had other results of an entirely different character but of the greatest importance to the development of American womanhood and the ideals of American life.   The general public of the early eighties was not so familiar with the story of poverty in the large cities as it has since become, and the contact with poverty-stricken childhood, incompetent motherhood, and homes that were

hardly such even in name brought to many women a revelation of existing social conditions that was nothing less
than startling. "The story of the slum was beginning to
be told," but its significance had not been realized. The
stirrings of the "social movement" were beginning to be
felt, however, and the desire to know "how the other half
lives" was awakening. No adequate agencies had existed,
however, by which that desire could be gratified, —
slumming parties belonging to a later date, — and no
satisfactory means had seemed to be at hand to relieve
the conditions which were said to exist. The kindergarten association seemed therefore to meet the need of
the hour. It afforded opportunity in part for the acquaintance with conditions that must precede intelligent
effort for relief, and furnished an agency by which an
amelioration of some of the conditions could be effected.
An idea of this phase of association work can be gained
from the following description by Miss Constance McKen-
zie of work done in Philadelphia during the early years
of the kindergarten movement.

"The touch of the kindergarten upon the home had
a humanizing effect which appeared nothing short of
remarkable. One short street, at that time reputed to be
among the worst in the city, was in some respects practically transformed by the home visits and the reflex influence of the kindergarten children. At the time when
the kindergarten began its unobtrusive crusade in that
neighborhood, to walk through the street meant to invite
an assault upon four of the five senses, as well as upon

one's sense of decency. The place and the people were filthy; the conversation was unfit to listen to; the odors were appalling. By and by, however, a change became noticeable. The newspapers, apologetic substitutes for glass, disappeared from many broken window-panes, and old cans, sweet with green things growing, took their places. Chairs were cleaned when 'teacher' was announced, and by and by the rooms were kept brushed up to greet her unexpected coming. After a while the children's work, first discarded as trash, began to assume an extrinsic value — the walls must be fresh to receive it. The children insisted upon clean clothes to be worn to kindergarten, and a general if dingy wash followed. In the evening fathers found a sufficient entertainment in the children's singing to keep them home from the grog shop; then the beer money was diverted, and found its way to the Penny Savings' Fund, through the child's little bankbook. The street people began to hush their talk as the kindergartner or the neighborhood visitor went by. The kindergarten children could be distinguished in the street, singing the songs and playing the games, and so potent was the effect of their small public opinion that their refusal to enter into the coarser street romps with the non-kindergartners brought many a child into the kindergarten who had been wont to stand at the door to hoot and run. Lessons of cleanliness, thrift, and trust were learned through experience and communicated to the homes through the insistence of the children and the friendly home talks of the kindergartners. The early stony indifference of the parents gave way to mild curiosity as to 'what the kindergartner would do next.' This melted into astonishment that she could make Johnny mind without using the strap. Then followed interest in John's gentler manner, compunction over his unconscious condemnation of the mother's way of doing things, and a shamefaced determination to do as 'the kindergarten teacher did,' until a new atmosphere pervaded many a home which at first sight had seemed irredeemable."

The face-to-face contact with social conditions which the work of a kindergarten association thus occasioned could not fail to awaken new interest and shape action in new directions. As the child study work had led association members into the field of general education and to an acquaintance with the leaders of educational thought, so the first-hand acquaintance with the problems of poverty led to a study of sociological literature and to a coöperation with philanthropists and social reformers. The interests thus developed have contributed materially to the growth of the social movement and to the advancement of philanthropy. Women have played no small part in the establishment of the newer forms of philanthropic work of the preventive and constructive kind, such as vacation schools, playgrounds, and social settlements. The kindergarten association was in fact a social settlement in embryo, and the kindergarten as such forms one of the chief agencies in the social settlement as it now exists.

The practical work for which a kindergarten association was organized could not be adequately carried on without the organization and maintenance of a training school from which its supply of kindergarten workers could be recruited. The successful management of a mission kindergarten demanded a kindergartner of experience and more than ordinary ability, but young women without previous experience or training and of a lesser degree of ability could serve in the capacity of assistants. The novelty and interest of the work led many young women to offer themselves as candidates for kindergarten training in the early days, not alone such as hoped to find in kindergartning the means of gaining a livelihood, but those who undertook the work from philanthropic motives only, and who expected no remuneration for their services. The work of the training course shaped itself to meet these conditions. Since workers were needed in the kindergartens and practical experience with the children must necessarily constitute an important part of the training, the candidates were assigned to actual work in the kindergarten from the time that they entered the course, and continued such work until it was finished. This necessitated the placing of all the studies of the course in the afternoon and in placing the emphasis upon the technical ones, — the mother plays, and the gifts and occupations. As the main purpose of these studies was to meet the immediate needs of the students in their work with the children, the work was of necessity fragmentary. As kindergarten training schools grew, instruction in music and drawing was added; later, courses in nature study, physical culture, and story-telling were introduced and, later still, courses in psychology, literature, and other subjects.

The establishment of kindergarten training departments in normal schools and other institutions in recent years has opened up a whole series of questions concerning the organization of kindergarten training courses. From the standpoint of pedagogical principle the apprentice form of training, which the exigencies of a kindergarten association necessitated, cannot be defended, and it has of late received no little criticism. The training of this character was the only form of training to be had until recently, however, as the private training schools were organized upon the same basis. What the instruction in such schools lacked in scholarship, however, it made up in other respects. Judged by the spirit of the kindergartner toward childhood and her skill in meeting its problems; by her enthusiasm for the cause under whose banner she had enlisted; and by her spirit of helpfulness toward those who needed help, the training was successful in its highest sense. The young women who took the training found in it both inspiration and help. It impressed upon them the need and value of preparation for motherhood, and the necessity for courses in domestic science and child study in women's colleges. The training received in the association training schools was an indirect training in philanthropy, and impressed the students with their moral obligation to childhood and to the community. That the work was felt to be valuable

F

is shown by the fact that many schools, organized originally to meet local needs, outgrew these and attained a wide reputation. Students came from enlarging areas, and graduates from the larger schools may be found in nearly every state in the union. The names of Mrs. Alice H. Putnam, Kate Douglas Wiggin, Patty S. Hill, Caroline M. C. Hart, Mrs. Eliza A. Blaker, and many others, superintendents of kindergarten associations and principals of association training schools, are known to every kindergartner in the land.

In building up kindergarten sentiment throughout the country perhaps no one person has done more than Mrs. Kate Douglas Wiggin, and the work of no kindergarten associations is better known that that of the two San Francisco associations identified respectively with the names of Mrs. Wiggin and Mrs. Sarah B. Cooper, now deceased. The kindergarten had gained a foothold in Los Angeles in 1875. One of the first young women to take a kindergarten course was Kate Douglas Smith, now known the world over as Kate Douglas Wiggin. When in 1878 the San Francisco Kindergarten Society was organized, Miss Smith was called to take the leadership. "That interest in the kindergarten grew under the direction of this gifted leader was but natural," says Miss Fisher in the Report of the Commissioner of Education. "No single individual has done more to spread kindergarten influence and to gain friends for the cause than the author of 'The Story of Patsy.' No kindergarten has enjoyed a wider celebrity and achieved greater success

among the children and in their homes than the celebrated
Silver Street Kindergarten, conducted by Mrs. Wiggin
and her sister, Nora A. Smith. The work done at Silver
Street was the mainspring of all subsequent work in
California."

The work so auspiciously begun by Mrs. Wiggin was
the stimulus to the organization of the Golden Gate
Kindergarten Association, identified in the public mind
with the name of its founder and president, Mrs. Sarah B.
Cooper. Mrs. Cooper was a woman of rare power and
influence, who had been identified with every phase of
philanthropic work, but whose great mission — "to lay
the foundation for a better national character by founding
free kindergartens for neglected children" — was revealed to her by a single morning's visit to the Silver
Street Kindergarten. Under her auspices a kindergarten
was organized and was supported by the members of her
Bible class. As the work grew, the association connected with her name was formed. Her influence brought
legacies and donations from many sources. No philanthropic association has supported so many kindergartens or expended so much money. The first legacy
of $20,000 was followed by an endowment fund of $100,000
from Mrs. Leland Stanford, who later contributed $20,000
more. Mrs. Phœbe A. Hearst was equally generous.
In 1891, $30,000 was contributed to this association alone;
in 1900 it was estimated that the association had received
in legacies and donations not less than $500,000. At
the time of its greatest prosperity it supported forty-four

kindergartens, and at the time of Mrs. Cooper's death, in 1896, it had conferred its benefits upon eighteen thousand children. The effect of such work upon the educational tone of California is incalculable.

The work of kindergarten associations in illustrating kindergarten ideals and methods, in organizing an effective means for the moral salvation of neglected childhood, and in securing the incorporation of the kindergarten into the school system, has been admirably supplemented by the efforts of individuals in different parts of the country. The work of some of these antedated the foundation of all but the earliest kindergarten associations, and doubtless stimulated their formation and growth. The first charity kindergarten in the United States was established in 1870, as has been stated, in connection with the Poppenhausen Institution at College Point, New York. The kindergartners employed were trained in Germany, and the provision was the most liberal in every way. In 1874 Mr. S. H. Hill, of Florence, Mass., contributed funds to open a charity kindergarten and later placed in trust a sum sufficient to sustain and extend the work. The largest and most significant individual charity in behalf of the kindergarten cause was that supported by Mrs. Pauline Agassiz Shaw of Boston, the daughter of Louis Agassiz. Having opened two kindergartens during the summer of 1877, and having satisfied herself of their value, Mrs. Shaw concluded that the kindergarten cause needed her support. "This was the beginning of a work unparalleled for public spirit and liberality and to which must be attributed the growth and final adoption of the kindergarten throughout New England," says Miss Fisher. Under the guidance of Miss Laliah B. Pingree, and supported by Mrs. Shaw's liberality, the kindergartens grew and prospered and became a power in the community. In 1883 Mrs. Shaw supported thirty-one kindergartens in Boston, Cambridge, and Brookline. No effort was spared to make these kindergartens the best of their kind. Through lectures by specialists on many subjects the kindergartners were provided with opportunities for advanced study. After supporting these kindergartens for ten years, Mrs. Shaw invited the school board of Boston to investigate their value and to consider their adoption into the public schools. As they had shown their value with the children, the board assumed the responsibility, and in 1888 kindergartens became an integral part of the Boston public school system. The report of the Boston School Committee says: "The wise and far-sighted generosity of these public-spirited women deserves to place them among the greatest benefactors of our schools. The school board has especially conveyed to them its grateful appreciation of their noble work, and the community which receives the benefit of all that they have accomplished should hold their memory in lasting regard." This in substance is the story of the kindergarten in Boston, as told by Miss Fanny L. Johnson, in *The Kindergarten Review*.

The city of Washington has also profited by the public spirit of a noble woman. Kindergarten effort at the

national capital dates back to the early years of the movement, but it has received special reënforcement during
the last decade of the century through the generosity of
Mrs. Phœbe A. Hearst. The introduction of the kindergarten into the Washington public schools is the result
of two influences, — that of Mrs. Louisa Mann, daughter-
in-law of the great educator, and that of the Columbian
Kindergarten Association, organized in 1893 for the
purpose of inducing Congress to effect legislation to that
end. Mrs. Hearst, Mrs. Cleveland, and several other
prominent women were active members of this association, and it was in connection with it that Mrs. Hearst's
greatest gift to the kindergarten cause was made. Her
donations to the cause had already been scattered far and
wide. Seven of the kindergartens of the Golden Gate
Kindergarten Association of San Francisco, and many
others in other western states, were supported by her.
Among her gifts to San Francisco was a perfectly equipped
building for training purposes. Her principal gift to
Washington was a training school, opened in 1897. The
home of this school was described by a recent writer as
attractive and artistic. It had an excellent reference
library, and the course of training was supplemented by
lectures given by the best specialists in the country. As
these lectures were open to the kindergartners of the city,
as well as to the students in training, the school became
the center of kindergarten interest in Washington. Mrs.
Hearst was obliged to withdraw her support from the
undertaking in 1905, but the results remain.

Although these contributions to the kindergarten cause are doubtless the most notable ones, many a city in the land can point to evidences of contributions as generous in proportion to the donor's means. Some of these donations have been made independently, while others have been made in connection with kindergarten associations, churches, or charitable organizations. The William N. Jackson Memorial Building, the permanent home of the Indianapolis Free Kindergarten Association, was a gift to the cause. Beautiful buildings for kindergarten purposes have been contributed to the cause also in Asheville, N.C., in Youngstown, Ohio, and in Spokane, Wash. In Topeka, Kan., a building for kindergarten purposes was given to a church which had organized and supported a kindergarten and training school. Memorial and endowed kindergartens are by no means uncommon. In 1903 Mrs. Leland Stanford supported six memorial kindergartens in San Francisco. The endowment fund of nearly $200,000 which Mrs. Stanford contributed to the Golden Gate Kindergarten Association has already been mentioned. "A generous friend of the children," who did not wish his name mentioned, recently gave $75,000 as an endowment fund for the Brooklyn Kindergarten Society. These instances are given as illustrations of what people of wealth and character have thought it worth while to do for the kindergarten movement.

Similar in general character to the work done for the kindergarten movement by kindergarten associations and individuals has been the work done by women's clubs.

Elizabeth Peabody, the apostle of the kindergarten movement, was a member of the New England Woman's Club,
the first club of the kind organized in the United States,
and at one of the earliest meetings presented the kindergarten as a topic in which women should be fundamentally
interested. Many other women prominent in kindergarten circles have been equally prominent in club organization and club effort. Miss Annie Laws, who was for
two years the president of the International Kindergarten
Union, was at the same time an officer of the General
Federation of Women's Clubs. Many clubs have made
a study of the kindergarten and others have taken the responsibility of kindergarten organization and support,
either independently or in connection with kindergarten
associations. Many facts of interest pertaining to the
work of particular clubs might be cited. The kindergarten established by the Woman's Club of Chicago was
declared to be "the nurse and feeder of the intellectual
and practical life of the club." The organization of the
General Federation of Women's Clubs has been a great
stimulus to work of this character, and the systematic
study of the whole field of education by that great body
promises much for the newer movements in education in
the near future. Mrs. Henrotin's report to the National
Educational Association in 1897 on "What Women's
Clubs have done for Education" contains some interesting
data. She reports kindergartens as having been established in several cities through the agency of women's
clubs, and systematic action having been taken to acquaint

the uninitiated among club members with the principles which underlie kindergarten procedure. The last object was accomplished at one state federation meeting by the setting apart of a day for the visiting of the kindergartens, and following this by a discussion of their value. In New Jersey, kindergartens were organized and supported through the agency of women's clubs until the school boards were sufficiently convinced of their value to adopt them as a part of the school system. The women's clubs of the District of Columbia appointed a committee to present to both houses of Congress a bill to make the incorporation of kindergartens into the school system possible. This has since been accomplished. In Colorado the adoption of the kindergarten into the school system of several cities has been effected through club agency. In Arkansas the State Federation has worked in connection with the State Kindergarten Association to secure the establishment of a kindergarten training school supported by the state. In Beloit, Wis., kindergartens were established and supported by the Woman's Club until the school authorities were ready to adopt them. The Woman's Club of Houston, Texas, has carried on a kindergarten for several years. Within the past few years the Southern Federation of Colored Women, of which Mrs. Booker T. Washington was then president, adopted the kindergarten as the chief line of work and study. In 1902 the colored Women's Clubs of Chicago organized kindergartens in several different sections of the city, locating them in the colored churches. At least nine kindergartens were thus established and supported. Whatever its immediate prospects the kindergarten movement may certainly hope for ultimate success, having such allies as the National Council of Women, the National Congress of Mothers, and the General Federation of Women's Clubs.

The value of these efforts of associations, clubs, and individuals can hardly be overestimated. In an editorial in *The Kindergarten Magazine*, when there were but seventy-five kindergarten associations, Miss Amalie Hofer said: "There are seventy-five thoroughly organized kindergarten associations in our states, all existing for the purposes of further study, for extending the work in new fields, or maintaining its sincerity in old fields. Some of these associations comprise prominent citizens who lend their influence and money to the movement; others are composed of kindergartners and teachers who meet under the Froebel banner for self-education; others consist of groups of earnest parents who are aiming to create public interest in this vital work of child training. These working centers form a network from city to city across our continent. The self-appointed stewards of the new education are a thoroughly organized force, six thousand strong, pledged to a modern reformation. The seventy-five officered kindergarten associations form a ganglia of vitalizing centers throughout our country and constitute what we name the kindergarten movement. These centers, each of which is illumined by the dedicated lives of strong, earnest, aggressive women, push their energies in many directions." The number of kindergarten associations has multiplied many times, and much has been accomplished for the kindergarten cause since these words were written. Women's organizations have done much to further the kindergarten movement, but other agencies still have contributed to its growth. The service that they have rendered will be discussed in succeeding chapters.

CHAPTER VI

The Period of Extension; The Kindergarten in Church, Sunday School, and Mission Work

It is no small testimony to the many-sidedness of the kindergarten that organizations differing widely in aim and character should have adopted the kindergarten as an agency for the furthering of their own particular aims. That the church should consider it a valuable means of carrying on its own work; that the temperance workers should hold it well-nigh indispensable; and that business firms should consider it a valuable phase of their welfare work, — these things cannot but surprise the uninitiated. Each of the agencies named has adopted the kindergarten to some extent, and has thereby become unconsciously a kindergarten propagandist. That kindergartners and kindergarten associations should advocate the kindergarten cause is not surprising. The acceptance of the kindergarten by the above-named agencies was, however, unlooked-for testimony to its value, and an unsolicited aid in acquainting the public with its principles.

Among the first of the above-named agencies to adopt the kindergarten was the church. One of the first churches of the country to adopt the kindergarten, if not the first, was Trinity Church of Toledo, Ohio, which in 1877 established a kindergarten as a part of its parish work. The Anthon Memorial Church of New York City, of which the Rev. R. Heber Newton was pastor, established a kindergarten in 1878, and the work done under its auspices is a striking example of what a church may accomplish through kindergarten agency.   While the adoption of the kindergarten by the church was slow during the early years, the movement was steady and quiet, as is shown by the fact that during the next decade kindergartens were established in several important foreign mission stations. The Golden Gate Kindergarten Association of San Francisco, organized in 1880, had its origin in a kindergarten supported by a Bible class connected with the Howard Presbyterian Church, under the leadership of Mrs. Sarah B. Cooper; and from that time on, until her death in 1896, Mrs. Cooper was one of the strongest advocates of this phase of church work.   The kindergarten has become an accepted agency in the institutional church, as it has in the social settlement which is akin to it, and the increase in the number of institutional churches has in a measure marked the increasing number of church kindergartens.   There are many churches that support kindergartens which are not strictly institutional, but as a rule the two go hand in hand.

That the kindergarten has become an agency in church and mission work, and that kindergarten principles are being accepted and applied in the Sunday school, is generally known, but little is known concerning the extent to which it has been thus adopted.   In the list of over four hundred kindergarten associations already referred to, over sixty are church associations. This does not, however, indicate the number of church kindergartens. In the same report, confessed as inadequate, since "a very great number of associations failed to respond to the request for information," Dr. Harris states that at least three thousand kindergartens not supported by public school funds are known to be in existence, although but about half of that number replied to the circular sent out. In a list of kindergartens compiled by Miss Clara Louise Anderson in 1903, inadequate also for similar reasons, the kindergartens not supported by public funds are divided into two nearly equal classes, those that are private in the sense that tuition is charged or that they are intended for a given class of children only; and those that are free, in the sense of being charitable or missionary in character. Supposing this proportion to hold in regard to the three thousand mentioned, there must be nearly fifteen hundred of the mission or charitable class. There is no known source of information from which the number of these supported by churches can be inferred, but there is evidence that three hundred would be a conservative estimate. A little definite information comes from Dr. Josiah Strong, of the American Bureau of Social Service. He admits that "no statistics concerning the number of churches throughout the country having kindergartens have ever been collected," but states that there are fifty-four such in Greater New York, twenty-seven in Philadelphia, and twelve in Chicago. A recent item in one of the kinder-

garten periodicals states that there are ten such in Louisville, Ky. From the data given by Dr. Harris and Miss
Anderson it appears that churches in fifty or more cities
support kindergartens as a part of their church work.
Every denomination seems represented, — the Roman
Catholic, the Lutheran, the Jewish, the Friends, the
Swedenborgian, the Unitarian, and the Christian Scientist,
as well as the better known Protestant denominations, such
as the Methodist, Baptist, Congregational, and Presbyterian. The Protestant Episcopal Church seems to be in
the lead in the number of churches supporting kindergartens. Among the conspicuous examples of churches
carrying on such work are: the Anthon Memorial Church,
already mentioned; St. Bartholomew's Protestant Episcopal, and the Manhattan Congregational of New York
City; the Every Day Church of Boston; the Central
Church of Topeka, Kan.; and the People's Church of
Kalamazoo, Mich. Of special interest is a Chinese
Presbyterian Mission Church in New York City that supports a flourishing kindergarten for Chinese children.

The auxiliary organizations of the church, such as the
Young People's Society of Christian Endeavor, or such
organizations as the King's Daughters or the Young
Women's Christian Association, have also in many instances
supported kindergartens. This seems to have been a
favorite form of effort for bands of King's Daughters to
undertake. In Peoria, Ill., there were at one time ten
such bands, eight of which directed their efforts toward
kindergarten advancement. In Syracuse, N.Y., the

Solvay Guild of King's Daughters rendered the kindergarten movement effective service.   Very successful work
has been done by this organization also in Des Moines,
Iowa, and in Knoxville, Tenn.   In Austin, Texas, a
colored band of King's Daughters did admirable work
in behalf of the kindergarten.   There are doubtless many
other places where such work has been done.   In Jamestown, N.Y., in Richmond, Va., and in Lansing, Mich., the
kindergarten movement was given its initial impetus by
the Young Women's Christian Association.   In Toledo,
Ohio, the Unitarian and Episcopal churches at one time
joined hands with the Women's Christian Temperance
Union and the local kindergarten workers to further
the movement.   In Birmingham, Ala., a kindergarten is
supported by a Young Women's Guild.   In Detroit a
kindergarten association has been organized by the Young
Men's Guild of St. John's Episcopal Church.   May
their names be blazoned abroad and their example widely
followed.   In 1902 the colored women's clubs of Chicago
established kindergartens in nine of the colored churches.
In Birmingham, Ala., the Baptist churches support two
kindergartens.   In several instances the work inaugurated
by the church or some other religious organization has later
been adopted by the public school authorities.   In New
Orleans the diocese supported a kindergarten and kindergarten training school for five years until the school
authorities were ready to assume it.   In Rochester, N.Y.,
St. Andrews Church for several years likewise supported a
kindergarten and training school, which the establishment

of kindergartens in the public schools later made unnecessary. The kindergartens of Toledo, Ohio, became a
part of the city school system after having been fostered
for several years by religious organizations. In Jamestown, N.Y., in Kalamazoo, Mich., and doubtless in many
other places public school kindergartens owe their origin
to church initiative.

The adoption of the kindergarten as a church agency will
be determined largely in any given case by the church's
conception of its mission in a large city. "In a city there
are two kinds of fields," says the Rev. Edward Judson in
his book "The Institutional Church." "In one the social
current seems to converge in favor of the church. Decent,
Sunday-observing, church-going people are living in the
neighborhood and all you have to do is to throw open the
doors of your beautiful church and the people flock in to
hear your fine preacher and your artistic music. Their
social life is not complete without a pew in the neighboring
house of worship. But there is another kind of field.
Who has not stood aghast and felt in despair as he has
stopped in one of our great thoroughfares and watched
the great tide of foreigners streaming ashore from some
emigrant ship; alien men, women, and children, chattering
in a strange language, and bearing uncouth burdens on
their heads and shoulders. They have come to stay. In
solid phalanx they take possession of wide stretches of our
city. They form an impregnable mass of humanity,
swayed by un-American ideas and habits. Our churches
retreat before this inflowing tide. But if our aim is to

G

change the character of our community, then we should bring to bear upon these masses our best Gospel appliances; our most effective measures will be preventive and educational, and our most enduring work will be with the children. The key to the hard problem of city evangelization lies in the puny hand of the little child." Dr. Judson speaks further of the Sunday school as "the church with its gearing adapted especially to work with little children," and pays high tribute to its power of reaching the children in such localities. "But the Sunday school alone is inadequate," he continues. "The sessions are too short and too far apart. Currents of sin and worldliness sweep between the Sundays and wash away holy impressions. What headway would we make in teaching arithmetic or geography if the lesson came once a week, occupied half an hour, and was taught by such incompetent, untrained, and unpaid teachers as are to be found in our Sunday school? If we would redeem the children the church must have her day school. Let her have a kindergarten which will embrace children from three to seven. These are too young to be admitted into the public schools and here is a providential opportunity which the church has of gathering them into her fold day by day. Let her employ a devout and trained kindergartner who shall not only educate the child's mind and body with the charming symbolic exercises of the kindergarten, but will tell each day a little of the story of the life of Christ, and teach the children Christian prayers and hymns."

Views similar to those expressed by Dr. Judson have

been voiced by Dr. R. Heber Newton and others. Dr. Newton has been one of the most earnest advocates of the kindergarten as a church agency. His faith was based upon the results accomplished in his own church. Not only was the effect of the kindergarten upon the children remarkable, but the influence of the kindergarten was extended and deepened by means of a training class and mothers' meetings until it was recognized as one of the most helpful means of building up the church and the neighborhood. The social settlement has found the kindergarten well-nigh indispensable, not only in building up character in the children, but also as a means of reaching homes that would otherwise be closed, and of bringing other members of the family under its influence. Had the church realized its social mission there would have been little need of settlements. These are doing what the church has too frequently failed to do, and they are suggesting ways and methods which the church would do well to heed.

But the kindergarten has a value not alone to the church of the kind described, but to the church on the avenue of the smaller city. Some of the most admirable examples of the church kindergarten are to be found among churches of this kind. One of the best examples of the kindergarten in church work is to be found in Topeka, Kan. The Central Congregational Church of that city organized a kindergarten as one of its working agencies in 1892. In discussing the step taken by this church the pastor, the Rev. Charles W. Sheldon, said: "When we consider the value to a church of work done for children by holding their growing life in close sympathy with church life and so educate future supporters of the church, it is surprising that the kindergarten has not found its way more quickly and generally into church activity. That this lack will soon be supplied in the city churches at least, the writer is ready to predict with much hopefulness." In describing the work of this kindergarten for *The Kindergarten Review,* Dr. Sheldon stated further: "An auxiliary composed of ladies of the neighborhood managed the details of expense. But the church considers the kindergarten as her own child, and is as much in touch with it as it is with the Sunday school which is carried on in the same room on Sundays. It may be said in this connection that all the young life of the church, the Endeavor Society and other organizations like it, center in this room together with the prayer circle of the church, and thus the room is constantly used and permeated with the spiritual energy which stamps all the work done there as distinctly and distinctively Christian.

"It is difficult to estimate the value to a church of regular kindergarten work carried on under its own roof," continues Dr. Sheldon. "The stimulus to the Sunday school, to the home, to the mothers, to every part of the church life, is instantly and continuously felt. It is the great hope and prophecy of the Central Church that other churches throughout the state will adopt this youngest child of Christian education, the church kindergarten. There is a positive advantage to any church to have its doors open every day of the week. But more than anything else is the immense value to all church growth and power gained from the daily presence within its walls and surrounded by its spiritual atmosphere, of the children who are the hope of the world and the future of the kingdom of God."

This kindergarten is an example for other church kindergartens in many respects. It has a model room of its own, a gift to the church from Mrs. T. E. Bowman, in memory of her husband. A training class has been carried on with marked success, and the kindergarten movement in the state has been materially advanced by the work it has done. The Central Congregational Church of Dallas, Texas, is organizing a similar work, and there are doubtless many other churches that could tell of like work successfully accomplished. The People's Church of Kalamazoo, Mich., has had a successful kindergarten in operation for several years. This was inaugurated during the pastorate of the Rev. Caroline Bartlett Crane, and under her leadership mothers' meetings were held and well attended. A special kindergarten is held during the Sunday morning service, that mothers who must either take the children to church or remain at home may have the benefit of the service. That the kindergarten as a phase of church work will increase in the near future can no longer be doubted. The tendency of the time is toward the establishment of institutional churches. In these the kindergarten will occupy an increasingly important place.

The reconstruction of religious thought that has been taking place in recent years has been discussed in a previous chapter. The acceptance of religious views akin to those of Froebel and the growing recognition of the social mission of the church have been influences tending to the adoption of the kindergarten as a church agency. But such reconstruction of thought has done more; it has revolutionized views and methods of religious instruction, and therefore affected the church's main agency for such instruction, — the Sunday school. The leaders of the kindergarten movement have been deeply religious, almost without exception, and recognizing that existing forms of religious instruction were at variance with the laws of the child's spiritual development, have from the beginning aimed at the improvement of Sunday school methods. The evidences of their success are apparent on every hand; the up-to-date Sunday school now has either a kindergarten department for children of kindergarten age or a primary department conducted externally at least on kindergarten principles. That the kindergarten Sunday school or the Sunday school kindergarten is wholly successful can as yet hardly be claimed. To substitute spiritual development for the traditional religious instruction in the Sunday school involved as great a change in Sunday school ideals and methods as the substitution of the idea of intellectual development for that of the traditional instruction in the school arts in the ordinary school work. In attempting such changes in Sunday school work, many mistakes have been made. Spiritual truths cannot always be expressed in material form, and the shortness of the Sunday school program will not permit of many

features that are permissible and proper in a day kindergarten.   Some of the kindergarten instrumentalities — the
songs, finger rhymes, pictures, and stories — are as valuable
and appropriate in a Sunday school kindergarten as in
any other, but it is a question whether the gifts and occupations have a place there.   The Sunday school teacher
who had the children sew a black heart to represent the
original sinful condition of that organ, and a white one to
show the effect of Christ's atoning sacrifice, had not yet
comprehended the true principles of kindergarten procedure in its application to Sunday school work.   If kindergarten training is necessary to carry on the ordinary kindergarten, it cannot be less necessary to carry on that highest
of all kinds, the church or Sunday school kindergarten.
As it is frequently impossible to secure a trained kindergartner, much of the so-called kindergarten Sunday school
work is form rather than substance.   That so much has
been done is occasion for congratulation, but it is only a
beginning.

The value of the kindergarten for the children and of
kindergarten training for the teacher is being increasingly
recognized in   missionary work — that among special
peoples in our own country, such as the Indians, Mexi-
cans, Negroes, and Chinese — and in the foreign field.
Information concerning the extent to which kindergarten
work has been so adopted has been difficult to obtain.
Some denominations appear to have taken up the kindergarten as a missionary agency to a greater extent than have
others.   The Roman Catholic Church has as yet done

little apparently in this direction, probably for the reason that teaching both at home and in the mission fields is confined to certain religious orders. The members of these orders would hardly be likely to have taken kindergarten training before entering upon the religious life, and could not do so afterwards unless the church itself were to establish a kindergarten training school. The Lutherans as a denomination seem to have done little toward the adoption of the kindergarten as a church or missionary agency. The Protestant Episcopal Church seems to have recognized the value of the kindergarten to an unusual degree, probably because it emphasizes the building up of Christian character from infancy.

The information on the subject of the kindergarten in missionary work given in the following pages is recognized as inadequate. It has been obtained from scattering notices in the kindergarten periodicals, from the missionary reports and magazines of some of the leading denominations, and from replies to letters. The field is not adequately covered, but all the information that was obtainable is given. Some conspicuous examples are given as illustrations of what is known to have been accomplished in some instances and of what may therefore be done in others.

That the demand for kindergartners in missionary work is constantly greater than the supply is a most gratifying symptom. A kindergartner who recently attended the sessions of the Executive Committee of the Women's Foreign Missionary Society of the Methodist

Church wrote to *The Kindergarten Review* not long since, as follows: "I met missionaries who were home from many different countries, and as I conversed with one and another, they almost unanimously expressed a present and instant need for trained kindergartners. From Japan, India, Peru, Mexico, and China come similar tales of efforts made to start kindergartens, where furnishing and materials were at hand, and pupils and native assistants eager to learn, but no competent, thoroughly trained kindergartners able to train native girls were in the field. Doubtless others had appreciated as little as I the special adaptability of the kindergarten idea in the training of little ones in the foreign lands, and the immense advantage which a kindergartner has because her methods may be easily applied without waiting to overcome the obstacles of language and custom which cause the teachers of older children to stumble most grievously. Now the thought that occurred to me, knowing that three of my own class in training were already in foreign lands, was this: Do the girls who are studying in our training schools and emerging year after year filled with the spirit of the child lover, intensified by the knowledge gained of ways of child gardening, know that other countries are pleading for the services which our country values so lightly because so easily obtained?" Kindergartners are hearing the call, "Come over and help us," from the foreign field with increasing frequency. At the Milwaukee meeting of the International Kindergarten Union there was an urgent call for a kindergarten training teacher to go to Tokyo to assume a position of great strategic importance, but the proper person could not be found. Miss Montgomery of the Oberlin Kindergarten Training School states that during the past five years she has had demands for kindergarten teachers for the foreign field which she has been utterly unable to supply. To meet such demands missionary training schools are establishing kindergarten departments in their institutions. Mrs. J. N. Crouse, of Chicago, president of the Baptist Woman's Home Missionary Board, stated in 1892, that she had found it advisable to provide at least partial kindergarten training for all the students in the Missionary Training School, and during the year fifty-six students in that institution had attended the mothers' meetings at Chicago Kindergarten College. The Baptist Training School for Christian Work at Philadelphia, and the Deaconesses' Training School at Grand Rapids, Mich., have adopted a like policy. The Folts Mission Institute at Herkimer, New York, an institution under the management of the Woman's Foreign Missionary Society of the Methodist Episcopal Church, has a regularly organized kindergarten training department of its own because of the need of trained kindergartners in missionary fields.

As has been stated, definite information concerning the number of mission stations that include the kindergarten has been difficult to obtain. The Woman's Board of Home Missions of the Presbyterian Church in 1906 made the following statement in reply to inquiry. "We heartily approve of kindergarten methods and kindergarten training, but as our work is almost entirely with exceptional peoples, we are unable to conduct many kindergartens. In our primary work we always give preference to teachers having the kindergarten training.   The gifts, the weaving, and the games are introduced into most of the schools under the care of Miss Goodrich in North Carolina.   We are hoping to establish a kindergarten in Havana, Cuba, next fall as a part of our mission work there.   I can assure you that the fact that we do not have many kindergartens in our schools is not due to our lack of interest in these methods of work, but rather to the demand for other work being so great that we have not had the funds for distinctive kindergarten work." The American Missionary Association of the Congregational Church, whose work is among the negroes, Indians, Chinese, and similar peoples, makes a reply to nearly the same effect. The Protestant Episcopal Church also has kindergartens in connection with its mission schools of this character. Kindergartens are maintained as a part of the mission work in the Hawaiian Islands and in Mexico also. The Presbyterian Board of Missions in 1896 sent a kindergartner to Bahia, Brazil, and the reports of her work have been most encouraging.

The kindergarten has become a part of the mission work in several different portions of Asia, Africa, and Australasia. The Woman's Board of the Interior of the Congregational Church maintains kindergartens in four out of its five mission stations in Benguella, Portuguese West Africa. The Methodist Episcopal Church supports at least one in Umtali, Rhodesia. Others are reported at Cisambia and

Bailundu, Africa, but by what denominations they are maintained could not be learned. There are kindergartens in the Samoan Islands, and at least one at Ruk, Micronesia. This was organized in 1897 by Miss Logan, whose father, the Rev. Robert Logan, gave his life to missionary effort in the Mortlock Islands. There is one kindergarten under the auspices of the Congregational Church at Kankesandurai, and another at Columbo, Ceylon. Several kindergartens are maintained in Burma by the Woman's Baptist Foreign Missionary Society. One of these is at Rangoon, one at Moulmein, and one at Bassein. This society also maintains a kindergarten at Mandelay, one at Huchow, China, and at least four in connection with its missions in Japan. In connection with two of these at Tokyo and at Kobe, training classes have been organized for the instruction of native girls.

The kindergarten has been adopted as an agency in the mission work in India by several denominations, but information concerning the extent to which it has been so adopted has been exceedingly difficult to obtain. A missionary recently returned from India is authority for the statement that the mission schools of all denominations are required by law to adopt certain features of the kindergarten in their elementary schools to secure certain privileges from the government. In the thirty girls' schools supported by the Foreign Missionary Society of the Methodist Episcopal Church in that country, these features are emphasized, and in several schools trained kindergartners are employed. A kindergarten department was organized in Thoburn College at Lucknow, the principal institution of the Methodist Church for the training of young women, ten or more years ago, in which many native young women have been trained. A kindergarten is maintained by the Friends Mission at Nowgong, Bundelkhand, and several are maintained by the Congregational Church. One of these is at Bombay, and another at Sholapur. At the last-named place a kindergarten training school has been organized under the direction of Miss Mary B. Harding, in which many native young women have been prepared for kindergarten work in other mission fields. Miss Harding has rendered an important service to the kindergarten cause in India by translating into one of the native languages the books collectively termed "The Republic of Childhood," by Kate Douglas Wiggin and Nora A. Smith. Calcutta, Cawnpore, Aligarh, and Madras are also known to be kindergarten centers, but the denominations under whose auspices the work was inaugurated and maintained could not be learned. Pundita Ramabai considered kindergarten training a necessary preparation for the work that she hoped to do for her own countrywomen. In the school which she established upon her return to her native country, in 1888, the kindergarten forms an important part.

China, too, is beginning to feel the beneficent influence of the kindergarten. Although little definite information could be obtained concerning the extent to which it has been adopted there, it is known to have become a part of the work of three great denominations,—the Baptist, the Methodist Episcopal, and the Congregational.

The kindergarten has become a conspicuous part of mission work in Turkey and in Japan, and an account of the work in these two countries cannot fail to be of interest. In 1896 there were twenty-eight kindergartens that had been established in Turkey by the Woman's Board of the Interior of the Congregational Church, and several that had been established through other agencies. The whole movement in Turkey grew out of the establishment of a kindergarten in the American School for Girls in Smyrna, in 1885. Miss Nellie S. Bartlett, who undertook the work there and who has seen it grow to its present proportions, thus spoke of it some years ago in *The Kindergarten Magazine:*

"The kindergarten was opened with seven children in the sunny room of the Girls' School. This proved to be the most attractive place in the building, judging from the eagerness with which the older pupils flocked to the windows and doors during the recess time. Erelong the room was crowded with thirty children, and still later as the number continued to increase, a part of them were accommodated in the chapel. It was a joyful day when the department was transferred to the beautiful building of the Woman's Board of Missions. The large hall is used for the general exercises and the Sunday school, and there are four airy class rooms. The training school is well accommodated here. In the pleasant garden each child has a small flower-bed to dig, plant, and water as he likes.

"The success of the Smyrna kindergarten created a

demand for a like blessing in other places," continues Miss Bartlett, "but this was out of the question without thoroughly prepared kindergartners. Hence young ladies from different parts of Turkey were sent to Smyrna for the needed training, which has been, and still is, a most important part of the work." In view of the importance of the work several additional American kindergartners were sent to Turkey. Miss Saunders, who was sent to Smyrna to assist Miss Bartlett, "was loaned to Constantinople after a year of faithful service, where in the midst of great difficulty on account of the condition of the country, she conducted a kindergarten training class and superintended several kindergartens by sending them plans of work." In Cesarea excellent work of the same kind was done by Miss Burrage, in Mardin by Miss Graf, in Van by Miss Huntington, and in Trebizond by Miss Halsey. Kindergarten training is carried on in the Girls' College at Marash by a native kindergartner, one of Miss Bartlett's graduates. Such training is also given in the Girls' Boarding School at Marsovan.

Miss Bartlett stated further that in the twelve years that had passed since the work was undertaken about fifty young women and two young men had taken a course in kindergarten training. The number of kindergartens had increased until at the time that the article was written, in 1896, there were twenty-eight, as has been stated, in Asiatic Turkey alone. A number of these soon became self-supporting. One, that at Yozgat, was supported by the local Y. P. S. C. E. Some of them received more or less help from America. All but two were carried on in the Turkish or Armenian language. English is used in the one connected with the American College for Girls at Constantinople, and the Greek children in the school at Smyrna are taught in their own language. Miss Bartlett concludes her article by saying: "If kindergartens are desirable in America, they are tenfold more so in this country. The kindergarten is now believed to be a necessity in every mission station and there is a greater demand for well-trained kindergartners than can be supplied."

Missionary effort in Japan has called the kindergarten to its aid with most gratifying results. "The time was," says a recent writer, "when missionaries worked mostly for grown-up people, but the children are getting their share, or a little of it these days, and kindergartens, Sunday schools, Young People's Societies of Christian Endeavor, and orphanages are helping to make life happier and better for the children of Japan." Kindergartens were established as a part of the Japanese public school system in 1876, and in 1904 it was estimated that there were one hundred eighty-two public and ninety-eight private kindergartens in the country. The very fact of the ready acceptance of the kindergarten by the Japanese people suggested their value as a missionary agency. In 1889 Miss Annie L. Howe, of Chicago, was sent to Japan by the American Board of Commissioners for Foreign Missions of the Congregational Church, to open a kindergarten and a kindergarten training department in Kobe College, one of the most important centers for the training of girls.

The kindergarten, called the Glory Kindergarten, was immediately successful and has more than realized the hopes of its founders. It now has two admirable buildings of its own, one for the kindergarten proper, and one a home for the students in training. The latter was the gift of Chicago friends, among whom was that stanch friend of the kindergarten, Mrs. E. W. Blatchford. A writer in *Life and Light* thus speaks of this kindergarten:

"The most fascinating place in Kobe, and I except not even the curio shops, the waterfall, or the walk over the hills, is the dainty little kindergarten which Miss Howe has mothered and which she is still mothering. Sight-seers come, and usually before they left England or America some one had told them to look up the kindergarten. But if, as sometimes happens, they do not know about it, some one here is sure to say: 'Have you seen the kindergarten? Then you must go.' And go they do, only to come away saying, as I myself heard at least two people say recently, 'It is the most fascinating place in Japan.' I have seen the kindergartens in Boston and other cities and enthused over them, but all in all I still commend the Glory Kindergarten." After commenting on the picturesque costumes and the exquisite manners of the Japanese children, the writer continues: "The rooms are large, airy, and sunny, and filled with every kindergarten necessity and many a luxury. Out in the yard each child has his own flower garden, which he cares for from the beginning, and his flowers adorn the school and go out to visit sick fellow-pupils. In winter each child has a plant and

H

this he cares for in true kindergarten style, with song and marching; and he learns its habits as he watches its growth, its budding, its blooming, and seeding from day to day. The children also have birds belonging to the school to care for, and in caring for them learn neatness and tenderness. Each child, too, at one time or another, has his pasteboard and gauze box containing silkworms, and these he feeds and watches through all their changes. In the cabinet in one of the rooms is a skein of silk spun from the children's own cocoons. It is not worth while going into further details. All that is done at home is done here, and they are not one whit behind in modern improvements."

Miss Howe herself thus speaks of the work: "When the children who go to the public school stand up to receive the certificate which they must take to their future teachers, they will feel, and we shall too, that a step upward has been taken. They will take with them the memory of the many prayers, the songs about God, the Christmas songs, the Bible stories they have come to know so well, the blessing asked at luncheon time, the ideas they have gained of the connection between flowers, fruit, grain, trees, — yes, and even stones, and the God who made all these things for us. They will keep on going to Sunday school, many of them, and I am sure that all this they have learned in a Christian kindergarten will influence them as long as they live." In 1904 she said: "Kindergartens which have won the confidence of the Japanese are very popular, and it is not unusual to have applications filed two years in advance, to secure a child's admission when he becomes

three years of age. A list of nearly two hundred applications has been known to be in waiting in October for
twenty vacancies which would occur in April, the time
when kindergarten children of six, according to Japanese
law, pass up to the elementary school."

In the first six years of its existence this kindergarten
had taught hundreds of children, the average attendance
being about seventy, and had graduated twenty-three
young women from the training course. The Congregational Church in Japan had in 1903 twelve mission
stations, and four of these have adopted the kindergarten
as a regular part of their work. All of these have buildings of their own and are well equipped. Dr. Gordon,
one of the missionaries, wrote as follows some time ago
concerning one of the Kyoto kindergartens: " It has been
my privilege to be associated with one (kindergarten)
established here in connection with our 'Airinsha,' or
House of Neighborly Love, our headquarters for philanthropic and evangelical work in the city. The printed
account of the origin of the Airinsha stated that the kindergarten had added much to the reputation of the house,
and promised to be one of its most permanent attractions.
Since then the kindergarten has marched right along on
the road to success, so that we have now one head teacher
and two assistants, and the limit of pupils that we have
set is entirely filled. This kind of work appeals especially
to the Japanese, and now that sentiment is not so favorable
to Christianity as it was a few years ago, I know of no
other method equally helpful in reaching Japanese homes.

The children are a delight to see. Nearly all of them attend the Sunday school and help to make it the success it is. The older brothers and sisters of the pupils, and in some cases their nurses, come with them to the Sunday school. The success of this kindergarten, as well as Miss Howe's good work in Kobe, has called attention to its importance." Here as elsewhere, in Japan and in other countries, the opportunities of the work are limited only by the lack of means and of teachers.

One of the greatest services that Miss Howe is rendering the cause of kindergarten advancement in Japan is the translation of Froebelian literature into Japanese. It is difficult to realize the difficulty of training kindergartners in a country where customs are strange, where the language is unfamiliar, and where there are no helps of any kind, — text-books, song books, or story books. "Miss Howe has a genuine Japanese mother-play book of which she is very proud," said a writer in speaking of her work in 1896. "She says, 'I have proved over and over again that Froebel's principles are as true in Japan as they are in Germany and America, and since the best kindergarten work is based upon that book, that book must be Japanned without delay. It is now finished.' In translating and publishing the book, a young man, Sadato San, was her invaluable assistant; and after nearly five years of effort it is safely through the press. The Japanese artist conformed the mother-play pictures to native canons and put in many pretty and suggestive touches of the life of Japan, yet he preserved the spirit of the subject wonderfully well. A song book adapting many kindergarten songs from Eleanor Smith's and other song books in use in American kindergartens has also been published in Japanese." Another such book has since been pubished, and in 1904 Froebel's "Education of Man," and several other books, had been translated and were awaiting publication. The preparation of these books will be of value to every kindergartner in the Japanese Empire.

The adoption of the kindergarten as a missionary agency in Japan will have a most important influence upon the character of mission work in the Orient, now that that nation has assumed the leadership in the Far East. In Japan, as in other countries where the kindergarten has been adopted, its value is twofold. It influences the children at an age when impressions are most lasting, and it proves to be one of the most effective agencies for reaching the homes of the people. For these reasons the social settlement considers the kindergarten one of its strongest agencies. The most successful church work at home and missionary work abroad is that which is adopting settlement methods. The Protestant Church is beginning to take to heart the lesson contained in a conversation reported by Julian Ralph. "Do the materialistic tendencies of the times weaken the Catholic Church in America?" I once asked of a Paulist Father whom I met on a railway train. "Oh, no," said he; "we Catholics catch our people young and they never get away from us. We hold that if we can have the care and guidance of a child under seven years of age, it will always come back to the church in after years, in every important crisis of grief or joy in life.   That is why our great church is unaffected by the godlessness that alarms others.   We make Catholics of little children, and they never cease to grow as the twig is bent."

CHAPTER VII

The Period of Extension; The Kindergarten in Temperance, Settlement, and Welfare Work

THE adoption of the kindergarten by religious organizations of different kinds brought it to the attention of many people who might not otherwise have made its acquaintance. It was brought to the notice of a still larger class through its adoption by the temperance workers of the country. The Woman's Christian Temperance Union must therefore be given an important place among the agencies that have aided in advancing the kindergarten cause. This organization has been conspicuous for its efforts to correct the evils resulting from the liquor traffic, and to reform lives and homes blasted by the drink habit, yet it has realized fully that the ultimate foundation for temperance must be laid in education, and the value of its educational work — less conspicuous than its corrective efforts — has been beyond estimate. The organization felt that intemperate husbands and fathers must be reclaimed and poverty-stricken, discouraged mothers helped to a higher plane, but that if the homes of the future were to be safe, the mothers of the present, whether the victims of intemperance or free from its blighting touch, must be taught such methods of child training as will make their children safe against the temptations of the lower senses. It felt also that mothers must be awakened to their responsibility for the kind of education provided in the school, and to the need of coöperation with those who are working for its improvement.

With these ideas in mind, the W. C. T. U. marked out two special lines of work that had an important bearing upon kindergarten progress. To acquaint mothers with the fundamental principles of child rearing as these are embodied in the theory and practice of the kindergarten was one; to stimulate them to effort in the direction of kindergarten advancement, such as the incorporation of the kindergarten into the school or the establishment of mission kindergartens in localities where the drink habit had worked the greatest havoc, was another. These lines of work could not be successfully carried out, however, without carefully organized effort, and the coöperation and leadership of kindergarten experts. The need of a kindergarten department in W. C. T. U. work was therefore felt, and such a department was subsequently added to those already organized. Since the work with mothers was felt to be of the greatest importance, a carefully planned course of study in Froebelian literature was outlined, and local unions were urged to organize classes for systematic work in this direction. The movement was undertaken with much enthusiasm all over the land, and its influence and value cannot be overestimated. As a means of creating sentiment in favor of the kindergarten nothing better could have been devised. Existing kindergarten literature was made the basis of the work done in these study classes, and the W. C. T. U. itself published several valuable pamphlets on the subject. Mrs. E. G. Greene, who occupied the position of Superintendent of the Kindergarten Department of the National W. C. T. U. during the eighties, issued a pamphlet of directions for local workers, called "Golden Keys," which is a complete manual on the subject. It gave the reasons why the W. C. T. U. had taken up the kindergarten as a department of its work, the aims of the department, the list of books to be read, and suggestions for conducting the local study classes.

No less valuable for the kindergarten cause was the work done by the W. C. T. U. in establishing kindergartens. Owing to the fact that statistics concerning the number so established or still maintained have been difficult to obtain, some of the most important ones may have been omitted in the list given below. The Central W. C. T. U. of Chicago established such a kindergarten in Bethel Mission in 1883, and maintained it for years. The South Side Union also maintained one for years. Other cities in which W. C. T. U. kindergartens are known to have been established are: Evanston, Ill., Philadelphia, Pa., Grand Rapids, Battle Creek, and Big Rapids, Mich., Albany, N.Y., Springfield, Vt., Portland, Me., Balitmore, Md., Toledo and Youngstown, O., Minneapolis, Minn., Lexington, Ky., and Los Angeles, Lakeport, Berkeley, San Francisco, National City, and San Jose, Cal. In the last-named city the kindergarten was inaugurated by the W. C.

T. U. and later taken up by the public school authorities. The amount of work done by local, state, and national workers in securing the incorporation of the kindergarten into the school system cannot be ascertained or estimated. Suggestions concerning the methods of effecting this are frequent in W. C. T. U. literature. While Miss Mary E. McDowell was superintendent of the kindergarten department of the W. C. T. U., a department was edited in *The Kindergarten News* under the heading "W. C. T. U. Kindergartens." In this the following suggestions were made. "By offering to support a kindergarten in a public school building for a year you will be giving an ignorant public and an indifferent school board an object lesson which may result in the adoption of the system as a part of the school work." A later suggestion is to the effect that "Legislation needs influencing also." "Laws incorporating the kindergarten as a part of the state public system should be passed by every state." Such legislation was effected through the efforts of the W. C. T. U. in at least two states, — Vermont and Michigan, — in the former in 1887 and in the latter in 1891. The discussion of kindergarten work in local, state, and national W. C. T. U. conventions, the addresses delivered by the superintendents of the kindergarten department, state and national, the published reports of the work accomplished by the kindergarten department, added to the influence of the kindergartens established and the mothers' clubs conducted, combine to form an influence that to a greater or less degree penetrated to every city, town, and hamlet in the country. The kindergartners of the country owe to the W. C. T. U. a great debt of gratitude for the work that organization has effected in behalf of the kindergarten cause.

Among the newer agencies to acquaint the public with the kindergarten and its work is the social settlement. The growing desire to render needed social service was one factor in the organization of kindergarten associations and like forms of philanthropic effort. The desire to minister to those in social, intellectual, and spiritual need gave birth likewise to the settlement, — the agency that more than any other expresses the spirit of the present age. So akin are the social settlement and the kindergarten in spirit that several head residents of settlements were originally kindergartners, and several well-known settlements began as mission kindergartens and became settlements by the natural expansion of their work. This is true of the Neighborhood House in Chicago, of the East Side Settlement in Detroit, of the Neighborhood Settlement in Milwaukee, of Bissell House in Grand Rapids, of Kingsley House in New Orleans, and of several others that might be named. Other settlements are still in the process of evolution from the kindergarten stage. In Boston the day nurseries have grown into settlements. The kindergarten places emphasis upon the natural instincts of childhood, — upon its love of companionship, its desire for activity, its love for the beautiful, and its yearning for knowledge. The educational process as interpreted by the kindergarten consists in the direction and utilization of these instincts for the furthering of the child's intellectual and moral development. The settlement recognizes the validity of these instincts in children of a larger growth, and seeks to develop and direct them in like fashion. The settlement has therefore been termed a kindergarten for adults. It is the recognition of these principles that gives form and purpose to settlement work. Is the neighborhood in which it operates lacking in opportunities for social enjoyment? The settlement must provide means and occasions to meet that need. Is there intellectual hunger which the locality has no means of satisfying? Study classes must be formed and other avenues to knowledge opened. Is appreciation of art needed, and are standards in its expression lacking? Art appreciation must be awakened and cultivated by exhibits or class instruction, and by concerts and musical societies. Like the kindergartner, the settlement worker must find the point of contact in those with whom she is working and through spontaneous interest and active effort lead to an appreciation of fundamental truths and governing principles. The settlement has, as a rule, no dogma to inculcate, like the church; no doctrine to which it wishes to convert the public, like the kindergarten association, and no special purpose to accomplish, like the W. C. T. U. As the kindergarten furnishes an all-round development because it meets the child's varied needs, so the settlement aims to develop the community to which it ministers by providing for its many-sided needs. In this lies both its strength and its limitation. The settlement did not adopt the various forms of manual training for its clubs and classes from a desire to further the manual training movement, although it is aiding the progress of manual training as a factor in education. It did not teach art or music for the sake of advancing the cause of art education, although it is doing so most effectively. It did not include the kindergarten among its agencies from a desire to promulgate the doctrines of Froebel, although it is doing much for their acceptance. It recognized the kinship between the spirit and method of the kindergarten and those of its own, and adopted that institution as a perfect instrument for the accomplishment of its own ends. It has advanced the cause of the kindergarten, but in its own way. The settlement movement is not centrally organized. It has no machinery like the W. C. T. U. by means of which it can instill a given doctrine into the minds of the many. It has no work mapped out by a central authority which each settlement is supposed to take as a working guide. Each settlement is an independent unit, working in fraternal relation to other settlements, but acknowledging no central authority. And yet the settlement has rendered a great service to the kindergarten cause and to the cause of the new education. It has taken a strong hold upon the public imagination. Its residents, mostly young college men and women, are those who will aid in shaping the educational thought and practice of the future. The young men and women now in college, however, are still largely the product of the old educational régime, and the college ideal is still mainly the intellectual one. Since child study is not an integral part of the average college course, few college students have an acquaintance with the nature and needs of early childhood, or a knowledge of the new educational movements. Few of those who undertake residence in a settlement have come into working contact with a kindergarten, or with children's clubs, playgrounds, and vacation schools in which its principles are applied. That the aim of the settlement and that of the kindergarten are identical, that successful settlement work is that which is based upon the methods employed in the kindergarten — these are arguments in favor of the kindergarten that are convincing and unanswerable. The settlement may not have intentionally preached the doctrines of Froebel, but it has practiced them in every phase of its work. In the playground, the children's club, the vacation school, nay, in the very settlement itself, one may read the philosophy of the kindergarten writ large. The settlement has baptized many a college man and woman into a new spirit; it has given them a new insight into the meaning of education and of Christianity. It has lent an interest to work with children that is liable to be sadly lacking in college graduates. If it had done nothing more for the kindergarten than to introduce it thus to college people, it would deserve the gratitude of every friend of the kindergarten movement. But it has done more, — it is interpreting Froebel anew to the kindergartners themselves. At the Chicago meeting of the International Kindergarten Union, Miss Jane Addams told the kindergartners there assembled that if Froebel were to come back to earth he would be distinctly disappointed to find the kindergartners so largely occupied with children only, since his is a theory of life, and not of child education alone. The follower of Froebel who is not making the kindergarten a center for neighborhood work has not, in Miss Addams' judgment, grasped the whole significance of Froebel's doctrine. That she needs to look away from the details of kindergarten technique and study the social significance of Froebel's philosophy is the message of the settlement to the kindergartner of to-day. By its adoption of the kindergarten the settlement has interpreted it to the public in a larger and higher sense. It is the kindergartner's duty to see that the public is not disappointed.

It is of interest to know that the first two settlements opened in the United States, the University Settlement in New York and Hull House in Chicago, have had kindergartens from the beginning, and that nearly if not quite half of the two hundred settlements listed in the "Bibliography of Settlements" for 1905 include the kindergarten among their agencies. Here, too, incomplete returns make a complete statement impossible. There can be no question concerning the place that the kindergarten occupies in the estimation of Hull House. Its equipment for the work with children is exceptionally complete, and its Children's Building, erected in 1896, for the special use of the neighborhood children may well serve as a model for other settlements. It is four stories high, and contains completely equipped club rooms, a nursery, a general playroom, and a kindergarten room that is a model of beauty and convenience. The superintendent of the nursery is a trained kindergartner who also superintends the games and plays, the playgrounds, the children's clubs, and all matters pertaining to the child life of the neighborhood. The kindergarten has been at different times in the hands of the most choice and talented kindergartners of Chicago. One of the oldest kindergarten training schools in the West, that conducted for more than thirty years by Mrs. Alice H. Putnam, gathered its students under the Hull House roof for several years, in the conviction that the contact with the social conditions of a settlement would add to the practical value of professional kindergarten training. Other settlements too have served the kindergarten cause in this manner. The classes of the Chicago Kindergarten Institute met for several years at the settlement conducted under the auspices of the University of Chicago, and Chicago Commons is the permanent home of the Pestalozzi-Froebel Training School. In giving the kindergarten students an insight into child life in large cities and in acquainting them with kindergarten principles in this larger interpretation, these settlements have rendered an additional service to the kindergarten cause.

Closely allied to settlement work in many respects is the welfare work now being undertaken by many large business firms with the coöperation and for the benefit of their employees. Employers are beginning to recognize — apart from any moral concern that they may feel for those in their employ — that clean and wholesome conditions of labor will attract a better class of workers and produce more and better work than will the opposite; in consequence, a general improvement in factory conditions is taking place. Attractive lunch and rest rooms are being provided, factory grounds are being beautified, educational facilities are being offered, and wholesome and helpful recreation is being furnished. The benefit does not as a rule extend beyond the employees themselves excepting indirectly, but in several conspicuous instances direct provision has been made for the welfare of the families of the employees, and in some cases such benefit has been extended to the community. Herbert H. Vreeland, Chairman of the Welfare Department of the National Civic Federation, says: "Realizing that men could not do their best work unless their homes were what they should be, classes in domestic science have been organized to teach the proper preparation and serving of food, how to buy groceries, the desirability of cleanliness in the house, and how to make comfortable and economical clothing. It goes without saying that a good wholesome meal will make a more contented and efficient workman, and that the disappearance of slovenliness from the household will make the fireside an attractive and winning competitor of the saloon when the day's work is over." The National Cash Register Company of Dayton, Ohio, maintains "a model cottage such as working people can provide for themselves, which serves as an object lesson of how to make such a home pretty and attractive." It

I

is presided over by a deaconess and operates as a sort of social settlement. This "House of Usefulness," as it is deservedly called, has indirectly taught many a lesson in home making and keeping, and has been of the greatest service in many ways.

To increase the happiness and efficiency of the worker, provision must also be made for the welfare of his children. Playgrounds, gardens, clubs, and classes of different kinds have therefore been provided in several instances, to occupy the hours that the older children spend out of school, and kindergartens have been established and maintained for the benefit of the younger children. The National Cash Register Company already mentioned has maintained for several years a kindergarten in which a hundred or more children are enrolled. The author of "Factory People and Their Employees" describes the work of this company at some length. He says, quoting the reasons given by President Patterson, of the company named, for the establishment of the kindergarten: "An employer of a large number of men owes it to himself to obtain the very best men possible, and to his employees to give them and their families every opportunity for their best development. If the city in which the factory is placed does not itself offer complete forms of education, then it is within his province to set an example showing what can be done by the best schools. His purpose in carrying out these ideas is not to do these things permanently but to show his own city their value." This Mr. Patterson has done so fully, in the judgment of the author quoted, that the city of Dayton now has a complete system of kindergartens, all the result of the example of the kindergarten connected with his factory. The author quoted adds: "Mr. Patterson believes that he is in business not for a few years but for many, and that the difficulties of the past in obtaining workmen with bright ideas may be overcome by training the children of the present. Since 92 per cent of them will earn their living by manual labor, it is certainly proper to give them that early training which will make them the best workmen when they are grown. In short he expects his factory to need skilled labor and more of it for many years to come, and thinks that it is wisdom to assist in preparing for the future. He finds, too, that even so-called unskilled labor gives better service when the early training has been along right lines." "He also recognizes," continues the author in question, "that in his efforts to win the good-will of his operatives nothing will be more successful than opportunities given to the children of these men. Men of all classes appreciate what is done for their sons and daughters more than any other favors shown. Thoughtfulness, therefore, on the part of the employers for the families of the operatives must receive large returns in more kindly feelings on the part of the men themselves. Experience, not only in this factory but in others, has proved this to be a true statement of the purpose of this work."

The kindergarten conducted by this company is held in the model cottage mentioned. In it the children's clubs and classes also meet, as well as the cooking and sewing classes, the kindergarten association, the women's guilds, and other associations. So valuable does President Patterson consider kindergarten training and the kind of education of which it is the type, that a rule has been made that after 1915 no one shall be employed in the factory who has not had kindergarten training. Such endorsement of the kindergarten by practical business men is worth much to the kindergarten cause, and it cannot fail to call the kindergarten to the attention of others, either as a feature for adoption in the welfare work of business firms, or for adoption into the school system of such cities as have not yet given it consideration. That the action of the National Cash Register Company has done much to further educational progress in the city of Dayton cannot be questioned. It has not only set the seal of its approval upon the kindergarten, but upon manual training, gardening, and playgrounds, which are its legitimate outgrowths.

The business firm that must be awarded the banner for the extent to which it has adopted the kindergarten as a feature of its welfare work is the Colorado Fuel and Iron Company, of Pueblo, Col. This company owns forty properties consisting of coal, manganese, and iron mines, and coke camps, in Colorado, Utah, Wyoming, and New Mexico. It employs about fifteen thousand men, speaking not less than twenty-seven different languages. It carries on a completely organized system of welfare work, the outgrowth of a kindergarten started in one of the mining camps in 1892 by Mrs. J. A. Kebler, the wife of the general manager of the company, who afterward became the president. This was before the legislature had enacted a law making the maintenance of public kindergartens possible. The success of this first kindergarten was such that others were soon opened, with which certain features of welfare work were connected. This phase of work has grown until there are thirteen kindergartens in as many localities, each the center of work of the social settlement type. The company has organized a department called the sociological department, which carries on a complete system of work for the social betterment of the sixty thousand or more people that it reaches. The company received a gold medal at the St. Louis Exposition for the exhibit of the kindergartens in its mining camps, and several other medals for other features of its work.

The work of this company is unique in many particulars, and deserves the highest commendation from many standpoints. It recognized the importance of education for its employees and their wives as well as for their children, and it has therefore taken an active interest in the schools of the forty different communities in which it operates. These communities are mostly small towns of from five hundred to four thousand inhabitants, in which, through the coöperation of the company, the school has become the social and intellectual center to an extent that would delight the advocates of the larger use of school buildings. The schoolhouses are built with this purpose in mind. They are two stories in height, and in addition to the class rooms, contain a kindergarten room and a hall, where the lectures, concerts, and social gatherings of the community are held. "The credit for building and inspiring these modern schoolhouses must be given to the Colorado Fuel and Iron Company, in whose camps they are found and at whose request they were built," says Dr. R. W. Corwin, the superintendent of the sociological department. "In a number of instances the plans of the buildings were furnished by the company, and when the school fund was inadequate the company advanced thousands of dollars for the erection and equipment of the structure. The buildings in the southern fields are likely to be models of all future schools in the coal camps."

This company has made a new application of the idea of making the school the center of its community life, in setting apart special houses for the use of the teachers. These serve a double purpose. Dr. Corwin says again: "One of the problems which has long confronted the department is that of providing for its teachers and workers permanent boarding places and rooms. It is desired furthermore to have some place in each camp which may serve as a model for camp housekeepers, and which may be a sociological headquarters and a center for social work. In view of these needs the company has set aside, or built in a number of camps, houses for distinctly sociological purposes. As many rooms as are necessary for the accommodation of teachers and workers are furnished, leaving the remainder of the house to a family for occupancy, so that the teachers may not live entirely alone. The furnishings of the teachers' rooms are thoroughly practical and sanitary, and are intended to serve as a standard of taste from which housekeepers may realize how much may be accomplished with comparatively small expenditure."

It is in these homes that many of the women's and children's clubs and classes are held. "At first the people seemed reluctant about coming to the house to receive lessons in cooking and sewing," says Dr. Corwin. "This feeling, however, soon wore away and they now begin to feel that the house is for their benefit as well as for the teachers. They are much interested in the furnishings, and take special care to notice the arrangement and quality of the furniture; the condition of the cupboards, dresser-drawers, etc. Such details as the folding of the towels, table linen, and bed linen are also particularly noted. The sanitary couch has caused much comment. Many have expressed a wish to have their houses papered just like the teacher's house."

But it is the work of the kindergartens themselves that is of the greatest interest. As stated, these are thirteen in number, and accommodate nearly if not quite five hundred children. Some of them are located in buildings erected especially for this purpose, but for the most part they have comfortable rooms in the public school. The enrollment varies from twenty-five to sixty-three. With one exception they have a morning session only, the kindergartner's time in the afternoon being given to club and class work with the older children. Of the work in the kindergartens themselves the superintendent, Mrs. Margaret Grabill, says: "Our constituency makes necessary a few noteworthy differences in methods from those of the ordinary kindergartens. Many of the children come to us with no knowledge of English. This makes the first work with them difficult, but it is astonishing how soon they learn to speak and sing. Because of the deficiency in language a greater degree of occupation and constructive work is given, since the children can imitate the teacher's work long before they can understand or follow language. An extensive use is made of pictures and objects. The kindergartner is obliged to employ more than the usual amount of rhythm and physical culture work, as the little bodies are stiff and untrained. Many more than the usual number of games are played, and here again the progress is remarkable. Much time has been devoted to nature study, illustrated by construction work, in many cases exceptionally good considering the little hands that made it. Fairy stories, patriotism, courage, kindness, and gentleness have been illustrated in this way, and also by free-hand cutting, drawing, and water coloring.

"In 1903 an exhibit of kindergarten work was made at the Colorado State Fair held in Pueblo, and the diploma awarded for the best work was given to our display. A much more complete display was sent to St. Louis, where it attracted considerable attention because of its unique character and excellent workmanship. Whole mining camps, farmyards, houses and barns, gardens, windmills, kindergarten rooms, four and five roomed houses, each room furnished appropriately, and all made by the little children, were among the features of the display."

The benefit that the children derive from the work of the kindergarten is not the only one aimed at in such work as this. "From two standpoints the kindergarten is a factor of more than average importance," says one of the reports. "Not only does it begin the all-round development of the child at the most impressionable period, but it is in this field the master key to the whole social betterment situation. The kindergarten has had far more success than any other institution in dealing with our foreign people. By careful and tactful visitation and invitation the kindergartner dispels suspicion and secures the patronage of all nationalities. It enables her to get into the homes and win the confidence of the mothers. Then mothers' clubs are formed. In one camp there is a club of fifty members. In another a child study club is successfully carried on. This is composed entirely of English-speaking mothers. In still other camps mothers' meetings are carried on, foreign mothers attending, and music and industrial work supplying the place of papers and discussions. In nearly every instance the foreign mothers have taken an interest in this social betterment work as far as they have been able to understand, and especially have the calls of the kindergartners and the little entertainments of the kindergarten children been instrumental in winning the way to their hearts." With such a variety of nationalities it is not strange that a knowledge of Spanish and Italian should be required on the part of the kindergartners.

One is tempted to dwell at too great a length upon the admirable work done by this company. "The spread of the kindergarten movement during the past twenty or thirty years had been a significant part in the educational life of America. But kindergartens in a mining community supported entirely by a mining corporation are, as far as we know, unknown outside the camps of the Colorado Fuel and Iron Company," says Dr. Corwin, with justifiable pride. The company thoroughly understands the principles upon which the kindergarten is based, and appreciates the fact that by its means from one to two years are added to the children's school life. Since at least 25 per cent of the camp children do not complete the eighth grade, this is of the greatest value. The work done by this company is an object lesson to the whole country of what may be done in an industrial community in the direction of educational and social betterment, by wisely directed humanitarian effort.

Within recent years the kindergarten has also been taken up by several of the cotton mill owners of the Southern states. Detailed information concerning these has been difficult to obtain. Among the mills in which kindergartens are known to have been established are the Elsas, and the Exposition Cotton Mills of Atlanta, the Millingham Mills of Columbus, Ga., the Avondale Mills in Alabama, the Richland, Olympia, and Granby Mills of Columbia, S.C., and the Pelzer Mills of Pelzer, in the same state. The Eagle and Phœnix Company has opened two kindergartens within the past three years, one in Girard and one in Phœnix City, each of which will accommodate seventy-five or more children. The building at Girard was recently described as elegant and attractive, an ornament to the part of the city in which it is situated. The interior is of Georgia pine and the furniture is of the same material and finish. It has the needed cloakrooms, a bathroom, an anteroom, and a raised platform in the main room for the accommodation of visitors. The provision for the comfort and happiness of the children is not confined to the building alone. An outdoor gymnasium, equipped with all necessary apparatus, and flower and vegetable gardens, give the children opportunity for play and exercise out of doors. The grounds are ornamental as well as ample, and serve as an ideal for the beautification of lawns and dooryards.

Judging from an item that appeared in one of the kindergarten periodicals shortly before these kindergartens were opened, the idea originated at least in part with the operatives themselves. It stated that "the Central Federation of Labor, composed of representatives of all the labor unions of Columbus and of the Alabama suburbs of Phœnix and Girard, is planning with the aid of Mr. George J. Baldwin, a prominent Savannah capitalist who has extensive interests in Columbus, to start a kindergarten for the children of the working population. This is, so far as known, the first attempt made anywhere by trades' unions to promote an educational idea." In these kindergartens, as in others of the kind, the company pays all the expense, the salaries of the kindergartners included. Other business firms that are known to support kindergartens as a part of their welfare work are the Solvay Process Company, of Syracuse, N.Y., the Illinois Steel Company of Joliet, Ill., the Plymouth Cordage Company of Plymouth, Mass., and the Bardeen Paper Company of Otsego, Mich. With the present interest in welfare work, the example of these firms will doubtless be followed by others in the near future.

The adoption of the kindergarten by these different agencies, religious, philanthropic, and educational, has been of the greatest value to the kindergarten and to education in general. It has interested thousands of women in education that would not otherwise have made a study of educational problems. It has given them nobler conceptions of motherhood and childhood, and acquainted them with the fundamental principles of child training. The connection with an organization interested in kindergarten advancement has broadened the range of many women's interests. It acquainted them with the problems of the city, social, economic, educational, and religious. It showed them the need for philanthropic effort, and led them to an appreciation of the character that such effort should assume. It awakened many to the appeal that beauty makes to a little child and, as a result, to the value of art in popular education. It did much to bring about the acceptance of the new educational ideals and undoubtedly influenced the character of education in women's colleges.

As to the kindergarten itself, one can only guess what its present status would have been had not the influence of these different agencies — the church, the settlement, and others of a like character — been exerted in its behalf. The footsteps of its progress would have been slow indeed to all appearances, had it depended upon the school alone. It would have lacked, also, the many-sided interpretation that has made it a significant influence in American life. The church has called attention to the religious aspect of its doctrine; philanthropic organizations have called public attention to its social significance; and the school has pointed out the educational value of its underlying principles. But each is a part of the whole, and in emphasizing the different aspects of the Froebelian doctrine, each of these agencies has aided in interpreting the whole. It is the Froebelian doctrine in its entirety that is making the kindergarten the influence in American life that it is to-day.

But these facts, which are gratefully acknowledged by every intelligent kindergartner, should not blind the student of the movement to certain disadvantages that have resulted from the adoption of the kindergarten as a philanthropic agency. One of these disadvantages arises from the close connection that has been established in the public mind between the kindergarten and the crèche or day nursery. The two have frequently been established together, both serving a philanthropic purpose.

In consequence the kindergarten is regarded by thousands as being little if anything more than an advanced form of the day nursery, whose purpose is served if the children are kept clean, happy, and off the streets. Many mission kindergartens unfortunately justify this impression. The large number of children frequently enrolled, — much too large for effective work, — the economy exercised in the use of material, the low salaries paid, — these and other conditions that too frequently prevail in philanthropic work, have done much to obscure the real educational value of the kindergarten. In speaking of the kindergarten as a charity agency, and having in mind the conditions mentioned, Professor Earl Barnes says, "A silver spoon may be a very good instrument to scrape an iron kettle with, but it is very hard on the spoon."

The deterioration of the kindergarten itself under the conditions too frequent in the charity kindergarten and the obscuring of its educational significance to the public are not the only disadvantages arising from its adoption as a charity agency. The mission kindergartner often undertook her work as a labor of love and asked for no remuneration. If salaries were paid they were wholly out of proportion to the services rendered. The kindergartners' services therefore did not reach a true valuation in the educational labor market. When the kindergarten became a part of the public school system this occasioned difficulties that in many places have not even yet been satisfactorily adjusted. Salary conditions are improving in the kindergarten world, but many kindergartners are still suffering from the conditions that first determined the salaries paid.

The adoption of the kindergarten as a charity had another result from which the kindergarten of the present is suffering. That the kindergarten training could not be other than superficial when the purpose of the organization that provided it was fundamentally philanthropic has been elsewhere stated. The standard of entrance could not be high under such conditions, or the number of students would be too small to carry out the philanthropy in question. The training teacher or teachers employed could not be of the best, as the conditions of the treasury made it impossible. The time for theoretical training must be limited, since the students were needed for practical work in the kindergartens. In consequence many poorly trained kindergartners were sent out. To bring kindergarten training out of the condition which gave it its present form, and to place it on a level with training given to other teachers, is one of the pressing problems in the kindergarten to-day.

The disadvantages which the kindergarten has suffered from its adoption by some of the agencies named are, however, more than offset by the advantages it derived from such adoption. Had it not been for the kindergarten association, the church, and the settlement, the circle of those to whom the kindergarten is known would have been a limited one; as a result of the efforts of these agencies, it is known to every person of intelligence throughout the country. In this and other respects too many to be enumerated the services which philanthropy and religion have rendered the kindergarten cause cannot be overestimated and kindergartners everywhere are grateful that their beloved institution has been deemed worthy of such support.

CHAPTER VIII

The Period of Extension; The Kindergarten and Educational Organizations and Exhibitions

The growing appreciation of the kindergarten during the first few years of the new decade recorded in the last chapters was mainly outside of the teaching ranks. It was natural and fitting that the doctrines of Froebel should appeal first to mothers, and proof of their fundamental value that such was the case. But a movement of such vigor and power could not fail to make an impression upon educators, and even if they had turned a deaf ear to kindergarten appeals, the insistence of the kindergarten advocates within the teaching ranks, coöperating with the body of enthusiasts in the larger world, would eventually have compelled them to listen. The increasing Froebelian literature, the growing approval of kindergarten theory, the proved adaptability of the kindergarten to public school conditions, and the increasing emphasis upon the æsthetic element in education, — all these were influences tending toward its ultimate adoption by the school.

But the educational leaders themselves began to take steps to bring the kindergarten before the teachers of the country. The educational press and educational organi-

zations — state and national — have played a most important part in advancing the kindergarten cause. At
its first meeting in 1872 the National Educational Association had presented the doctrines of Froebel to the consideration of the American educational public, and before
1880 the cause of the kindergarten had been given several
hearings before that body. But something more was
needed than an occasional presentation of the kindergarten
on the general program, and at the meeting at Madison,
in 1884, steps were taken by which a kindergarten department was created. This was an important step for both
kindergarten and general education. The program of
the National Educational Association had not been of
such a character as to attract kindergartners to its meetings, and such meetings as the kindergartners had held
themselves had been attended by few if any of the teachers
and superintendents of the country. The organization
of the kindergarten department of the National Educational Association was therefore an important step in
taking the kindergarten out of its isolation and giving
it a place in the general educational system. If the kindergartners hoped for the ultimate adoption of the kindergarten by the school, they needed to acquaint themselves
further with school problems and conditions and if the
school was to incorporate the kindergarten into the general
system of education, the teachers needed an added familiarity with its aims and methods. What better means
could be devised to acquaint each with the purposes of
the other? At the first meeting of the department at

Saratoga, the president, W. N. Hailman, thus stated the main purpose of those who had taken the initiative in bringing about its organization. "To secure a thorough testing and sifting of kindergarten principles and methods, and to devise ways and means for the full and generous application of what may be found valuable and available in the educational work of the school. The efficiency of the kindergarten in the unfolding and filling of child life in its earliest stages has been brought to the petitioners (for the creation of the department) so unmistakably, that they yearn to secure for the school the powerful and beneficent influences involved. The chief problems which they hope the kindergarten department to solve are:

First: What are the principles and methods by which the kindergarten arouses even in little children, so deep, broad, and generous an interest in life and the things of life? How does it at so early a period in child life secure that thoughtful mastery of self and surroundings which is the root of all character and efficiency in life? How does it secure that rounded and complete living that neglects no faculty, strains no faculty, does violence to no faculty, but leads them all into a healthy growing activity that makes life consciously worth living at every step?

Second: To what extent do these principles and methods apply to the period of school life?

In the twenty-two years that have passed since the organization of the department, the National Educational Association has met in the following cities, in the order named: Saratoga, Topeka, Chicago, San Francisco,

Nashville, St. Paul, Toronto, Saratoga, Milwaukee, Washington, Asbury Park, Denver, Buffalo, Los Angeles, Charleston, Detroit, Minneapolis, Boston, St. Louis, New York, and Los Angeles. The benefit of these meetings to the kindergarten cause is simply incalculable. The importance of the occasion and the character of the audience has stimulated every kindergartner who has appeared on the program to her very best effort. The cause of the kindergarten has been strengthened in every community in which the meetings have been held, because of the presence of the leaders in the movement. The thousands of programs sent out and reports published have familiarized the public with every phase of kindergarten effort. Opportunity has been afforded the kindergarten leaders to become personally acquainted with the men and women who are shaping the direction of general education. To the Association it brought the stimulus of fresh and vital problems; the reënforcement resulting from the influence of a new and enthusiastic body of workers; and a general increase in educational intelligence and interest. The reports of the early meetings indicate that the car of kindergarten progress did not always move as smoothly and rapidly as its friends could have wished. "The new department was forced to work its way in the midst of great discouragements, outside as well as inside the educational profession," said one writer. "It was brought, like all similar reform movements, face to face with prejudice, skepticism, ignorance, and ridicule. It held its own, however, from year to year, presented an annual program to its members, gaining here a little more respect, there a trifle more encouragement and vantage ground. One by one progressive educators paused in passing by the kindergarten door to hear what was being said inside." But the interest continued to grow, and at the Nashville meeting the attendance is said to have exceeded that at the general meeting. In connection with the Toronto meeting the department was spoken of as the live department of the Association. The kindergarten did not fail to utilize the increasing interest, and the cause prospered.

During recent years the kindergarten cause has been materially strengthened in the South by the addition of a kindergarten department to the Southern Educational Association, the second largest educational organization in the United States. The first meeting of the newly organized department was held in connection with the meeting at New Orleans in 1898. Other meetings of that body have been held in Memphis, Richmond, Columbia, S.C., and in other of the larger Southern cities. The program of the kindergarten department has been most excellent in every case, and the influence of the meetings upon the growth of kindergarten sentiment in the South has been very marked. They have brought into prominence the kindergarten workers of the South, who have been too far removed from the kindergarten centers in other sections of the country to be adequately known and recognized.

The Saratoga meeting of the National Educational Association in 1892 is a memorable one in the annals of kindergarten history, since it was at that time and place that the International Kindergarten Union was organized, — now the third largest educational organization in the country. This was brought about as a result of a two-fold need. The first was that of a greater consolidation of the growing kindergarten interests than even the National Educational Association could offer; and the second was the making of a convincing presentation of the kindergarten cause at the approaching Columbian Exposition. The official report of the organization of the International Kindergarten Union reads as follows: "At the time of the thirty-second annual meeting of the National Educational Association held at Saratoga Springs, in July, 1892, a meeting of kindergarten training teachers, presidents of kindergarten associations, and others actively interested in the kindergarten movement, was held in the Baptist Church on the morning of July 15th to consider a proposition made by Miss Sarah A. Stewart, of Philadelphia, to make some formal organization of the kindergarten interests throughout the country and also to prepare the way for a fitting representation of this department of work at the Columbian Exposition in 1893. It was unanimously resolved at this meeting that such an organization was desirable and that a committee of seven be elected by ballot to take the matter under further consideration; to prepare plans for the organization, and to report at the afternoon session of the kindergarten department of the National Educational Association. The committee consisted of the following members: Mrs. Ada Marean

Hughes, Toronto; Miss Angeline Brooks, New York City; Miss Sarah A. Stewart, Philadelphia; Miss Mary C. McCulloch, St. Louis; Miss Annie Laws, Cincinnati. The remaining two members who were elected, Mrs. Sarah B. Cooper, San Francisco, and Miss Lucy Wheelock, Boston, were unfortunately absent.

At the afternoon session of the kindergarten department, the report of the committee was read by the chairman, Miss Stewart, recommending the organization of a National Kindergarten Union which would in no way antagonize the kindergarten department of the N. E. A. but would act in sympathy and harmony with it, only extending the field of work more widely than the department of the N. E. A. had as yet been able to do. The report was accepted, and it was decided to form a temporary organization to further consider the matter. Miss Stewart was made chairman and Miss Laws secretary of the temporary organization.

After some discussion it was decided that an association be formed under the name of the "International Kindergarten Union." The aims of the Union were to be as follows:—

1. To gather and disseminate knowledge of the kindergarten movement throughout the world.

2. To bring into active coöperation all kindergarten interests.

3. To promote the establishment of kindergartens.

4. To elevate the standard of professional training of kindergartners.

The special aim for 1893 will be to give as complete an exhibition as possible of kindergarten progress in the world, at the Columbian Exposition.

The officers elected were, — President, Mrs. Sarah B. Cooper, San Francisco; First Vice President, Miss Sarah A. Stewart, Philadelphia; Second Vice President, Miss Laliah Pingree, Boston; Corresponding Secretary, Miss Caroline T. Haven, New York; Recording Secretary, Miss Mary McCulloch, St. Louis; Treasurer, Miss Eva B. Whitmore, Chicago.

In commenting upon the step taken, Miss Hofer, of *The Kindergarten Magazine*, said: "Great credit is due Miss Sarah Stewart of Philadelphia, who so ably proposed and outlined such action, and who, as temporary chairman, carried the proceedings of organization in the most creditably parliamentary manner. Mr. W. E. Sheldon, of Boston, was also largely instrumental in securing so strong a plan of organization, having offered many valuable and practical suggestions. It is due to his foresight and knowledge of the minor details of the Association at large, that the Union placed itself in the proper relation to the N. E. A., as well as to the World's Auxiliary Congress, to both of which it must needs be subject in its efforts to push the educational exhibit of 1893." The work done through the combined efforts of these organizations will be discussed under another heading.

The I. K. U. thus owes its immediate origin to the stimulus of a great occasion, but the recognized need of an organization of the kindergartners of the country to

further the general interests of the kindergarten movement would doubtless have led to the formation of such
an organization at no distant date. There had been two
earlier organizations with aims almost identical. The
first of these was the American Froebel Union, which
was organized in Boston in 1877 by Miss Peabody. It
had held several meetings in Boston and one in New York.
In Detroit in 1879 a Western Kindergarten Association
was organized, the meetings of which were held in Chicago
and Detroit alternately. The organization of the kindergarten department of the N. E. A. in 1884 had, however,
seemed to make the continuance of these organizations unnecessary, and for eight years the N. E. A. meetings had
furnished the means of furthering the progress of the kindergarten movement, which had been the avowed purpose
of both. The kindergarten cause had made great progress
during these years, and the newly formed I. K. U. started
on its career with a promise of success and influence that
would have been impossible to the earlier organizations.

During the year following the Columbian Exposition
no meeting of the I. K. U. was held. In 1895 it was an
affiliated body with the National Council of Women on
the one hand, and with the N. E. A. on the other, and a
meeting was held with each of these organizations during
the year. The first was held in Washington in the early
spring. The National Council of Women devoted one
day to this department, which took its place as one of the
great national bodies which compose that Federation.
The leading kindergartners of the country addressed large

and appreciative audiences upon subjects of kindergarten interest. At the meeting of the N. E. A. at Denver, "the regular kindergarten department of the N. E. A. proved so very full and interesting under the able management of Miss Amalie Hofer," says the secretary, Miss Stewart, "that the I. K. U. seemed in danger of losing its separate existence. However, a grand rally was made at the close of the convention and very stalwart work was done in the line of business."

The secretary says, further: "The crowded condition of the programs of the N. E. A., owing to the large and growing number of its departments, made it seem necessary to appoint a separate time and place of meeting for the I. K. U. The Denver meeting forms the point of departure. It takes its place in the history of the organization only as a business meeting, where the effort was made simply to make time, and to appoint strong officers to organize and maintain a separate existence. Whether the separation from the two large bodies with which it had been affiliated was wise or unwise, as a settled policy, remains to be seen."

The first occasion at which the I. K. U. met as a separate organization was the meeting held at Teachers College, New York, February 14, 1896. This was the first meeting at which the general work for which it was organized was taken up, and its present working machinery evolved. It was a meeting of a handful of leaders only, but it was fruitful in suggestions for future work. The meeting at St. Louis the following year was the first of the larger meetings which have since come to have a value for the kindergartner in the ranks as well as for the leaders who are shaping the course of kindergarten prog ress. This meeting was made memorable by the presence of the Baroness von Buelow-Wendhausen, the niece of Froebel's foremost disciple and co-worker.

The succeeding meetings of the I. K. U. have been held as follows: In Philadelphia in 1898; in Cincinnati in 1899; in Brooklyn in 1900; in Chicago in 1901; in Boston in 1902; in Pittsburg in 1903; in Rochester in 1904; in Toronto in 1905; in Milwaukee in 1906; and in New York City in 1907. The growing numbers and the increasing size of the meetings have given it an added importance in recent years, and it is now ranked as the third largest educational organization in the country.

That the I. K. U. has done much to give unity, dignity, and momentum to the kindergarten movement all will admit. The adaptation of the kindergarten to American life and education was no simple problem. Experiments were being made in different sections of the country, by independent workers, under conditions totally different. An all-round development of the kindergarten idea could be secured only by a comparison of these experiments. A premature and one-sided crystallization of kindergarten interpretation and procedure could only be avoided by the same agency. The I. K. U. furnished the opportunity for comparisons; it acquainted each with the work that others were doing. The kindergarten of the future is being slowly evolved from the comparison of these experiments, and not the kindergarten only, but a complete system of primary education grounded in the principles of Froebel. In furthering this evolution the I. K. U. has rendered a lasting service to the kindergarten and to general education. But it has done more. It has unified, strengthened, and dignified kindergarten training. It has brought increasing inspiration to the kindergartner in the ranks by the increasing value of its meetings. Much remains to be done along the lines of investigation and propagation, and though the kindergarten department of the N. E. A. and the I. K. U. have rendered magnificent service in furthering the kindergarten movement, neither can as yet rest upon its oars in the satisfaction of labor accomplished.

Among the many agencies for bringing the kindergarten to the attention of the public, the summer schools that have sprung up everywhere of recent years must be given an important place. These have been of many kinds and have met varying needs. Some have offered instruction in some one line; the curriculum of others rivals in complexity that of the modern university. At the head of the list stands Chautauqua. To some Chautauqua is little more than a beautiful summer resort; to others it is a place for intellectual stimulus and recreation; to still others it is the opportunity for quiet, purposeful study. When, in 1879, Chautauqua added its "Teachers' Retreat" to its many attractions, it set into operation a most effective agency for influencing the educational thought of the country. For here teachers could see and hear the leaders of the new educational gospel, here they could acquaint themselves with the new methods that were growing in favor in every progressive community; here many saw a kindergarten in operation for the first time, and realized the difference between its spirit and method and that in vogue in the school. A kindergarten department was added to the educational attractions of Chautauqua in 1881, and as the local Chautauquas, now three hundred or more in number, were organized, they too included the kindergarten in their list of agencies for popular instruction.

The Chautauqua kindergartens serve a double purpose. Even if they had not been established for the purpose of instruction in the newest form of educational procedure, they would have been organized as a practical necessity. Chautauqua aims to provide enjoyment and profit for all who enter its gates, and shall the children who frequently must accompany their parents be denied their share in the generous provision? Kellogg Hall is as popular with Chautauqua children as is the Hall of Philosophy with adults, and the kindergarten circle is always filled. The children are not the only ones to be found in the kindergarten rooms. Every available space is occupied with the mothers of the children, members of the observation or training classes, or with casual visitors. Here is a mother from a distant state eager to have her child enjoy the advantages of the wonderful institution of which she has heard and read so much. There sits a minister from a Western city who had intended to stay through the opening exercises only, but who has forgotten the flight of time in his interest. In a corner sits a young woman recording every detail of the morning's work. She has come all the way from South America. "The Chautauqua plan is perhaps farther reaching in its effects than any other, since the entire country contributes its spectators," says a recent writer, and even the slightest acquaintance with the scope of work at any of the larger Chautauquas will demonstrate the fact that as a missionary agency for the kindergarten cause, it is unequaled. In addition to the kindergarten proper, there are classes for at least three groups of people. There is always a class for mothers, some of whom come for the special purpose of getting the help they need in the work with their children. There is a course for such kindergartners already trained, who wish a broader outlook and the opportunity which the occasion affords of interchange of views with fellow-workers. And last but not least is the observation class, which includes teachers and not infrequently ministers who wish to acquaint themselves with kindergarten procedure and the principles that underlie it. Chautauqua brings many interested and interesting visitors from all parts of the world. Among the many present during one summer the following were reported as belonging to one or the other of the three classes: a young woman from South America who at one time had charge of a kindergarten in the gardens of the Emperor of Brazil; a kindergartner from one of the leading cities of Canada who wished suggestions for enlarging the scope of her work;

the principal of a colored school in the South; a kindergartner from India; a home missionary from New Mexico;
a teacher in a government Indian School in Indian Territory; a missionary from China; a young woman from
South Africa; and the principal of a state normal school.
A list as varied and interesting could doubtless be compiled
each season. It is because of the presence of such people
that a course for kindergartners in normal schools and
primary and kindergarten supervisors has been organized
of late for the consideration of the larger kindergarten
problems.

The advantages which Chautauqua offers to mothers,
kindergartners, and teachers are not confined to the work
of the kindergarten department only. The provision
made for grade teachers is as ample as that made for
kindergartners and mothers, and many courses are offered
which are of equal interest to all. Courses in educational
psychology and child study, in children's music and in
art in the kindergarten and primary grades, given by
specialists, attract both kindergartners and teachers and
broaden the views of both. Primary teachers acquire
a knowledge of the kindergarten almost unconsciously,
since modern methods in primary work are based upon
kindergarten principles. The work at Chautauqua
has, perhaps, more than any other agency, introduced
the kindergarten to ministers and Sunday school workers
of the country. Froebel's views concerning the child's
spiritual nature are being increasingly accepted, and in
consequence more wholesome methods of religious in-

struction have come to prevail. Through the Chautauqua lectures and conferences on the problems of the child's spiritual development and the application of kindergarten principles to Sunday school work, kindergarten departments are becoming the rule in the Sunday schools of the country, and religion is taking its true place as a means toward the child's highest development. In all these ways Chautauqua must be considered as one of the great influences in furthering the kindergarten movement.

The kindergarten cause in the South has been materially advanced during the past six years by the establishment of the Summer School of the South, at Knoxville, Tenn. In addition to the kindergarten which is in session for the entire six weeks it has provided courses in child study and kindergarten literature for kindergartners and primary teachers, and holds kindergarten and other conferences for the discussion of problems relating to kindergarten work. In 1905 a Southern Kindergarten Association was formed for the purpose of discussing the problems peculiar to kindergarten work in the South and making plans for its more general introduction in that section.

The many summer schools of methods, held in different sections of the country during recent years, have been among the indirect means of advancing the kindergarten cause, and frequently the direct means as well. The first of these was Martha's Vineyard Summer Institute, the Mecca of progressive teachers for many years. Dexter says of this, "It must be placed second only to the great assemblies at Chautauqua in the breadth of its influence and the number of students who have attended. During its history nearly every educator of note in the country has appeared upon its platform." Kindergarten speakers always occupied a place on its programs. In 1885 the Saratoga National Summer School of Methods was organized. This was later combined with a similar school held at Round Lake, N.Y., and later still with the one at Glens Falls, N.Y., where it continued its work until 1897. The Cook County Summer Normal, at Chicago, was of the same character. Like Chautauqua, these schools drew the progressive and aspiring teachers by the courses of improved methods in teaching the common school branches, and by the opportunity afforded for acquaintance and conference with other progressive teachers. The leading kindergartners of the country gave lectures and courses of work, and the principles of the kindergarten were recognized and applied in the methods of teaching grade work. The summer school held at La Porte, Ind., by Professor and Mrs. Hailman, aimed directly at this. In this, as well as in several other summer schools, direct and special courses of instruction in kindergarten work as such were given. This was true of the summer schools held under the auspices of the Chicago Free Kindergarten Association, of the Chicago Kindergarten College, of the Grand Rapids Kindergarten Association, and several others. Through attendance at these schools thousands of teachers and school principals gained new educational ideas and an insight into the new educational doctrines. Though the work done could not

L

but be superficial in many instances, the summer schools must be considered as an influence of great value in furthering the new education.

The service that expositions and exhibits of kindergarten work could render the cause of kindergarten progress was recognized by the experiences of the Philadelphia Exposition. Since that date the friends of the movement have not been slow to avail themselves of the opportunities that have presented themselves. One of the first opportunities utilized was the Madison meeting of the N. E. A., already mentioned as marking a milestone in kindergarten progress. This was the first time in the history of the N. E. A. that an organized exhibit of school work had been made, and the kindergarten exhibit was "one of the most extensive and complete which has ever been made of kindergarten work," says the N. E. A. record, "a surprise to every one." The work of the kindergarten exhibit came from eighteen different cities, and comprised a wide range of institutions. The system that was seen to underlie kindergarten work impressed every one, and many additions were made to the roll of its advocates. Exhibits of school work have been among the most interesting and instructive features of the succeeding meetings of the N. E. A., and the kindergarten has been more or less adequately represented at each one. The I. K. U. has made intermittent and spasmodic efforts to have an exhibit of work in connection with its meetings, but in the judgment of many it has not risen to its opportunities in this respect.

The matter of an exhibit has too frequently been left to the ambition of individual workers, cities, or training schools, and there has been no concerted effort to secure a general representation of kindergarten work, or to bring the work of different schools of kindergarten interpretation into comparison. This is one of the directions in which the I. K. U. can profitably direct its energy in the near future.

The great expositions that have been held in the different sections of the country during the past quarter century have furnished many opportunities for acquainting the general public with the merits of the kindergarten, and in the case of the Chicago Exposition, at least, these were most admirably utilized. The New Orleans Exposition in 1885 furnished the first of these occasions. A kindergarten was conducted by Mrs. Anna J. Ogden and Miss Mary Crosby, both of Washington, during the entire period that the exposition was in session, and attracted great and favorable attention. A kindergarten exhibit had also been prepared, but the organization of educational exhibits on a large scale had not received the attention at that time that it has received since, and the exhibit was not so organized and placed as to attract the attention that it deserved. The kindergarten and the exhibit combined did much to awaken kindergarten interest, however, in the South particularly. As a result of the effort made, and of the place given the kindergarten on the program of the International Congress of Education held in connection with the exposition, one of the friends of the kindergarten cause said that "the kindergarten as such had been clearly raised from its former questionable isolation into the genial and friendly companionship of established educational forces."

What the New Orleans Exposition accomplished in behalf of the kindergarten for one section of the United States, the Columbian Exposition at Chicago did on a large scale for the whole country. The I. K. U. was organized, as has been stated, for the purpose of coöperating with the Board of Lady Managers in devising a plan that should accomplish the purpose desired. No adequate presentation of the kindergarten could be made that did not portray it in its relation to the whole life of the child from the modern-day standpoint. A most comprehensive plan was therefore formulated, which is indicated in part from the official circular, which read as follows: "Although the world has known many large expositions at various times in its history, in none of these have the interests of children received the full representation that they deserved. Such great progress having been made during the present century in the methods of educating, amusing, and caring for the physical well-being of the coming men and women, it seems desirable that an illustration of the best methods should be so grouped that they may be easily assimilated by, and made useful to, the vast number of people who will visit the World's Fair. In many cases it will be impossible for the mothers to visit the exposition without taking their children, and in so doing they will wish the little ones as well as themselves to take the fullest advantages of the educational facilities offered. With these ends in view the Children's Building has been designed, which will give to mothers the freedom of the exposition while the children themselves are enjoying the best of care and attention."

The beautiful Children's Home, "built by the women of the world for the world's little ones," was ninety by one hundred and fifty feet, and perfectly adapted to the purposes it was intended to serve. The ground floor contained the reception rooms, an assembly room, a completely equipped gymnasium, and several nursery rooms; and the second the kindergarten room, a manual training room, a court for a playground, and several other rooms. " Thinking of the myriad miles of bare schoolroom walls that belt the country, and are daily gazed at by thousands of impressionable school children, the committee sought to give illustrations of appropriate art for children; consequently, on ceiling, window, frieze, and panel were pictures of child life and pastime, or representations of the world-old stories that all children love to hear." The decorating of the interior of the building was put into the hands of kindergartners, the making typically beautiful the Children's Palace, and displaying the possibilities of wall decorations, for school and home, being considered a part of the occasion.

In the building was presented the best thought on every phase of child life. A series of manikins was shown, to represent the manner of clothing infants in the different countries of the world, and demonstrations were made of the most healthful and natural methods of feeding, dressing, and caring for children, according to modern scientific theories. The nurseries were models of their kind, and gayly decorated booths showed the toys and games of all nations. Stereopticon talks upon foreign countries were given to the older children by trained kindergartners, who then took them in groups to see the exhibits from the countries in question. The younger children were taken charge of in the beautiful kindergarten rooms, and the mothers given an opportunity to see a real kindergarten in operation. The Kindergarten Literature Company had its headquarters here, and distributed much valuable information concerning the kindergarten. Another opportunity to see a kindergarten in operation was given in the Illinois State Building, where a kindergarten was conducted for the entire six months by the joint effort of the two kindergarten associations of Chicago, the Froebel Association and the Free Kindergarten Association. "Two equally great purposes are to be served in the public presentation of the kindergarten at the World's Fair," Miss Amalie Hofer had said in *The Kindergarten Magazine.* "First, the attention of the world at large is to be called to the fact that the new education is operative, and the public is to be shown what it is and does. Second, the facts illustrating what it has already accomplished are to be arrayed before those already intelligent on the subject." The Children's Building was one of the means of accomplishing both purposes. Visiting kindergartners and teachers were invited to make the building their headquarters while at the exposition, and the opportunity for observation which it afforded, combined with the lectures there given on different phases of child culture, gave to many a teacher an entirely new view of child life and of the educational process.

The Children's Building furnished one of the means of acquainting the public with the new gospel of childhood. The exhibits and the congresses furnished others. At the time the educational exhibits seemed quite wonderful, although the better organization of such exhibits at the St. Louis Exposition reveals their crudity and lack of organization. The kindergarten exhibits were generously sprinkled in among the general school exhibits, some of them isolated, and others in relation to the school work of which the kindergartens formed a part. The casual visitors could not fail to be impressed by the frequency with which the kindergarten announced its presence. That it had come to stay was evident; that it had made its impression upon grade work was equally evident. The kindergartner learned many lessons by seeing her own work in its general educational perspective. The school principal and grade teacher could not but marvel at the general progress of the kindergarten movement. The student of educational progress who had seen the kindergarten exhibits of earlier years, could not fail to note that great influences were at work in the kindergarten world. The larger free work that appeared in some of the exhibits seemed ugly and inartistic to many in contrast with the small exact work to which they were accustomed. Others saw in this work a prophecy for the future. The evidences of the new movement have been accumulating in recent years, and discussions concerning it wax warm in kindergarten circles. But of this, more later.

To many kindergartners the educational congresses furnished the crowning inspiration of the exposition. The I. K. U. held a department meeting in the World's Congress of Representative Women, to set forth its own work and to discuss topics connected with it. There were two kindergarten congresses under separate management, and varying largely in scope and character. The first of these was the special kindergarten congress, which held its sessions the week beginning July 17th. This was presided over by William N. Hailman. The second was the meeting of the kindergarten section of the International Congress of Education, held July 25th to 28th, under the auspices of the N. E. A. This was in charge of Mrs. Ada M. Hughes, president of the kindergarten department of the N. E. A. Both congresses brought an earnest body of workers from far and near, who spoke with sincerity and conviction. The Special Kindergarten Congress opened with a paper on Froebel and his work, by William N. Hailman. Among the topics and speakers during the week were the following: "Every mother a kindergartner," Mrs. Sarah B. Cooper, San Francisco. "The place of music in the kindergarten," W. L. Tomlins, choral director of the World's Fair. "The professional training of kindergartners," Mrs. Eudora L. Hailman, La Porte, Ind. "The relation of play to work," Miss Angeline Brooks, New York. "Froebel's religious views," a discussion. "The influences of home and school upon child character," Miss Constance Mackenzie, Philadelphia. "Elementary science teaching," Professor Edward G. Howe. "Physical culture," Baron Nils Posse and Margaret Morley. A full morning was given to the discussion of art in the kindergarten, Miss Mary Dana Hicks leading. For one day the kindergartners and the manual training and art teachers met in joint session. The subject "Symbolism in early education" was discussed by Mrs. Marion Foster Washburne, and other appropriate topics were presented by Mrs. Louise Parsons Hopkins of Boston and Professor James L. Hughes of Toronto. The closing session of the week was held on Sunday afternoon, when Miss Lucy Wheelock of Boston, Miss Anna Bryan of Chicago, and Miss Annie Howe of Japan discussed the relation of the kindergarten to church and Sunday school work.

The kindergarten section of the International Congress of Education held three forenoon sessions. The topics for discussion had been carefully outlined by Commissioner William T. Harris, under whose general direction the congresses were held. The general topic selected for discussion at the first meeting was "The essential characteristics of the kindergarten as distinguished from the primary school." Under this the following sub-topics were considered: "The gifts and occupations of the kindergarten."

"Should the kindergarten attempt to teach reading and writing?" "Should the games invented by Froebel be modified or added to?" "What is the place of song in the kindergarten and what degree of the dramatic element should accompany it?" These topics were discussed by Mrs. Alice H. Putnam of Chicago, Mrs. Sarah B. Cooper of San Francisco, Miss Sarah A. Stewart and Miss Constance Mackenzie of Philadelphia, Miss Mary C. McCulloch of St. Louis, Professor William N. Hailman of La Porte, and others. The topic selected for the second session was "Kindergarten training," the many aspects of which were discussed by Mrs. Eudora L. Hailman, Mrs. J. N. Crouse of Chicago, and others. The subject of "Symbolism" was selected for the last session, and was discussed by Miss Elizabeth Harrison of Chicago, Professor Earl Barnes of Leland Stanford University, Professor Hailman, and others present. No description of the congresses or of the exposition as a whole can convey an idea of the inspiration that the occasion gave to the kindergartners of the country. To the younger kindergartners just entering the ranks it was an inspiration to see and hear the leaders of their cause. To the older workers the enthusiasm of their younger sisters was the prophecy of what might be accomplished in the future. The extent to which the kindergarten had invaded the educational territory was a surprise to all and a promise of the ultimate surrender of the forces of conservatism in the teaching ranks. The kindergarten seed had been scattered broadcast, and they knew that the harvest would be forthcoming.   They had made a great effort.   The passing years have proved that it was not in vain, and that the kindergarten entered upon an enlarged sphere of influence from that date.

The work of the Chicago Exposition for the kindergarten cause was so thoroughly done that succeeding expositions have found it unnecessary to make a corresponding effort in its behalf.   The educational work done in connection with the Cotton States and International Exposition held in Atlanta in 1895 was of great value to the South, however, since the new education had not secured so strong a foothold in that section at that time as it had in other sections.   The educational committee, composed largely of Atlanta teachers, coöperated with the managers of the Woman's Building to erect a Model School Building and to maintain a kindergarten and a primary department during the time that the exposition was open.   The kindergarten was conducted by Miss Mary Hill of the Louisville Free Kindergarten Association, and the primary department by Miss Minnie Holman of the Peabody Normal at Nashville, Tenn. The exhibits of school work were of value, but the interest centered in the work done with the children.   The kindergarten was in the most conspicuous part of the Woman's Building, which in turn was situated in the most central and conspicuous part of the grounds.   In consequence, says a writer, "the crowds in the kindergarten were continuous; two or three hundred passing would step in for a while and then pass on, only to be replaced by a crowd equally large." It was unfortunate for the kindergartners and for the cause, however, that the children were those taken from a charitable institution, and that results were not what might have been hoped for. In spite of discouraging conditions, however, much was accomplished, and Miss Hill had occasion to explain the principles and methods of the kindergarten to hundreds of interested visitors.

The new education was well represented at the Trans-Mississippi Exposition at Omaha in 1898, although the kindergarten was not emphasized. The Exposition managers gave into the hands of the Omaha women all interests of an educational nature, the erection of the children's building, the organization of the school exhibits, and the management of the educational congresses. The kindergarten received its share of attention in each of these lines. It was not due to lack of interest on the part of the Omaha women, however, that more effort was not centered on the kindergarten, as they had tried without success to secure the I. K. U. meeting for their city on that occasion. They were successful, however, in securing the meeting of the National Congress of Mothers, and since the emphasis of its meetings was placed upon the study of childhood and the importance of training for motherhood, it accomplished much for the kindergarten indirectly. Among the speakers were several prominent kindergartners, Miss Caroline M. C. Hart of Baltimore and Miss Amalie Hofer, and Miss Frances Newton of Chicago, being among them.

The Pan-American Exposition at Buffalo in 1901 furnished another occasion for acquainting the general public with the kindergarten idea. The Buffalo Kindergarten Union utilized the opportunity and held a Kindergarten Convocation lasting for three days, July 1–3. It is not often that the president of a great exposition is also the president of a kindergarten association, but Mr. John G. Milburn, president of the exposition, who welcomed the visiting kindergartners and the many interested outsiders at the first meeting, spoke in the capacity of president of the Buffalo Free Kindergarten Association as well. The leading speakers were Dr. William N. Hailman, Miss Virginia Graeff of Cleveland, Miss Rosemary Baum of Utica, Mrs. Mary Boomer Page of Chicago, Mr. Percival Chubb of New York, and Col. Francis W. Parker. An attractive exhibit from the kindergartens of Buffalo added to the interest.

By the time that the Louisiana Purchase Exposition of 1904 was held, the kindergarten was no longer a waif seeking adoption into the educational family, but a child accorded full rights and privileges. The exhibits of the Palace of Education showed kindergarten work in its natural relations to other school work; the kindergarten took its turn with the cooking schools and manual training classes in exhibiting its work in actual operation; and the N. E. A. and other educational congresses gave it adequate recognition on their programs. In theory the battle for the incorporation of the kindergarten into the school system has been won; in practice much still remains to be accomplished. The great popular movements above mentioned have been noble allies and they will continue to do service in behalf of the kindergarten. But new problems are arising that call for new solutions. The discussion of these problems will be taken up in later chapters.

CHAPTER IX

The Period of Extension; Progress in Literature

THE literature of the kindergarten has been one of the sources from which the new educational thought has been derived. It struck a higher note in the gamut of education than had hitherto been sounded, and the whole educational symphony is being gradually modulated to the new key. Its beginnings have been noted, but an appreciation of its progress and influence requires a glance at the literature of general education. At the time that the kindergarten made its appearance in the United States the school was a dreary place, and it is not surprising that the literature of education, — what there was of it, — should have been lacking in inspiration and value. Barnard's *American Journal of Education* was established in 1855, and this, with a few other educational journals, devoted to the practical problems of school organization and administration, practically occupied the field. As early as 1860 Mr. Barnard published a series of books called "Papers for the Teacher," consisting of articles reprinted from the *Journal*, bearing upon the practical problems of the schoolroom. He also published separately in pamphlet form, many of the articles that had appeared in the *Journal*. With this exception, the only book of

direct value to teachers published before the Civil War
was Page's "Theory and Practice of Teaching." This
was published in 1847, and is of great value still. Until
education began to be considered as a process of development instead of a process of instruction only, no books
on elementary education were written. As has been
stated elsewhere, this change of view was due to the growing acquaintance with the principles of Pestalozzi, and
the center of Pestalozzian influence was the Oswego
Normal School. In this school and among its graduates,
sympathy with the joyous, overflowing life of childhood
began to take the place of the repression that had hitherto
prevailed, and the child's interest in the things of sense
began to be recognized as having an educational value.
An acquaintance with things began to be considered
a necessary preliminary to the teaching of words, and
objective teaching became the watchword of the new
thought. The "object lesson" became the center of
educational interest, and a course in object lessons was
scheduled in every progressive school curriculum and
program. This occasioned a demand for literature upon
the subject, and Dr. Sheldon's books on "Object Lessons"
and "Elementary Instruction," written in response to the
demand, were widely read both in the United States and
in England. Dr. A. E. Winship says in reference to Dr.
Sheldon's work: "A general desire to know about the
new ideas led to the preparation of the first books printed
in America upon the adaptation of Pestalozzian principles
to our school work. These books marked an era in

American education.   This was really the birth of educational literature in America." Calkins' "Manual of Object Teaching," published later, was a part of this same movement.

During the decade between 1870 and 1880 several additions were made to the literature of education.   Abbott's "Gentle Measures in the Management of the Young" was published in 1872.   This was of great value to mothers as well as teachers and did much to change the general attitude toward childhood.   In 1874 Professor William N. Hailman published his "History of Pedagogy," which gave to many their first insight into the historic development of the new educational views. His "System of Objective Teaching" was published soon after.   Two other books of importance were Wickersham's "School Management" and "Methods of Instruction."   Of the first of these, Dr. Winship says that it "was probably the best professional book issued up to that time, and remained a standard for a quarter of a century."   He adds the interesting fact that it is the only American professional book ever translated into Japanese and used by the government of Japan as the official book for teachers to study.   Both of these books were used as text-books in many of the normal schools of the United States for many years.

The stock of pedagogical literature was being augmented also from other sources.   Krusi's "Life of Pestalozzi" appeared in 1875 and Dr. Barnard's "American Pedagogy," "English Pedagogy," and "German Teachers

M

and Reformers," reprints also of articles that had appeared in the *Journal*, were issued soon after. Johonnot's "Principles and Practice of Teaching," published in 1878, was a book of great value. The educational literature of the present still leaves much to be desired, but its relative abundance compared with the scarcity of books before 1880 makes one forget how recent is the new educational thought, and how gradual has been its development. Probably no one person has contributed more to the transformation of education than Colonel Francis W. Parker, but his first work, "Talks on Teaching," was not published until 1883, and the pen pictures of his work at Quincy, Mass., under the name of "Quincy Methods," was not given to the public until 1885. The first volume of the International Education Series, Rosenkranz' "Philosophy of Education," was not published until 1886. In fact few if any of the books that for years constituted a part of every pedagogical library, —Rousseau's "Émile," Payne's "Lectures on Education," White's "Elements of Pedagogy," Fitch's "Lectures on Teaching," Compayré's "History of Pedagogy," W. H. Payne's "Contributions to the Science of Education," were available before 1885. "The literature of pedagogy is still in its infancy in the English language," said an educator of note in 1885. And so indeed it seemed.

Against this general background of pedagogical literature the increasing literature of the kindergarten is to be placed if it is to be rightly comprehended. It is astonishing but true that more books were translated and written

concerning the kindergarten during the decade between
1870 and 1880 than were translated or written on the
whole of general education besides. The progress in
kindergarten literature during the period following cannot fail to interest all who are interested in the progress
of education. The first notable contribution of the new
decade was Barnard's "Kindergarten and Child Culture
Papers," published in 1881, — a reprint, like his other
volumes, of articles that had appeared in the *Journal*.
Some important translations appeared during the decade,
— "Goldammer's Manual," an English translation of
the Mother Plays, by the Misses Lord, and Froebel's
"Education of Man," translated first by Miss Jarvis and
later by W. N. Hailman. This was the first volume of
Froebelian literature to appear in the International Series.
"The Hand Book of Froebel's System" was also translated, as was the "Autobiography of Froebel," the former
by Miss Wheelock, and the latter by Miss Emelie Michaelis
and Mr. H. Keatley Moore of London. Some of the
most important of Froebel's works were not translated
until after 1890. A volume of Froebel Letters was translated by A. H. Heineman in 1893. In 1895 the volume
of essays known as "Pedagogics of the Kindergarten"
was translated by Miss Jarvis, and the same year Miss
Blow made a new translation of the Mother Plays. This
was published in two volumes, the first of which was
entitled "Mottoes and Commentaries of Froebel's Mother
Play," and the second, "Songs and Music of Froebel's
Mother Play." The three volumes appeared in the

International Series, as did a later volume of essays, entitled "Education by Development," translated by Josephine Jarvis in 1899. Another volume of letters, entitled "Froebel's Letters on the Kindergarten," was translated by Miss Michaelis and Mr. Moore in 1896, and the translation and adaptation of Hanschman's "Life of Froebel" by Fanny Franks, known as the "Kindergarten System," in 1897. With the translation and publication in 1901 of the "Life of the Baroness von Buelow," written by her niece, the most important of Froebel's own works and those of his intimate successors have been made available to the English reading public.

The books above mentioned vary in value and popularity, but all have contributed something to the advancement of the new educational views. Some are of general educational interest and are therefore to be found in every up-to-date pedagogical library. Others concern themselves with the details of kindergarten procedure and are therefore of value to the professional kindergartner mainly. The general deepening of insight into the principles of the kindergarten among the great body of kindergartners has rendered the specific kindergarten manuals less necessary than they were in the earlier years of the movement, and has occasioned an increasing demand for the books that embody the fundamental principles of the kindergarten and of education in general. The "Mother Play Book" and the "Education of Man" are used as text-books in every kindergarten training school in the country worthy of the name, and the "Pedagogies of the

Kindergarten" and others are used as reference books in most of them. The first two have been translated into many languages, and are known the world over. Froebel's "Autobiography," the two volumes of "Letters," the "Life of Froebel," and the "Life of the Baroness von Buelow" are used in every class in the history of education that places emphasis upon the historical development of the new educational movement.

But the public has not depended wholly upon the works of Froebel himself for an acquaintance with the principles embodied in the Froebelian philosophy. One of the greatest services that the kindergarten has rendered to American education is the stimulus that it has given to original work. The kindergarten has been a fruitful theme for the essayist and author, and the list of books written within recent years as a result of kindergarten inspiration is a creditable one. Such books may be divided into two general classes, — those whose aim is the interpretation of the kindergarten, and those whose purpose is to discuss the development of childhood in general. These aims overlap in most cases, but the emphasis is usually upon the one or the other. Of the thirty or more books on the kindergarten written since 1880 not more than six appeared during the decade between 1880 and 1890. The new institution needed to be tested under the varying conditions of American life and education before its advocates could speak with the authority they wished, and those who were gaining the needed experience were at first too occupied with the experience itself to enter the field of authorship. Of the six books mentioned, Professor W. N. Hailman's "Law of Childhood," published in 1880, was the first. This was a series of essays that had appeared in *The New Education*. The second was Miss Peabody's "Lectures to Kindergartners," which was given to the public in 1886. This consisted of a series of lectures which for nine or ten years she had delivered before the kindergarten training classes in Boston and other cities.

The third book, published the same year, was entitled "The Kindergarten and the School." It consisted of articles by four active workers, on the relation of the kindergarten to the school. The fourth volume was "Conscious Motherhood" by Miss Emma Marwedel, published in 1887. This was an application of Froebel's doctrine to the development of childhood, based on such observations as had been recorded by Preyer in his "Mind of the Child." As the means of arousing an interest in genetic psychology among kindergartners, this book was of more than ordinary value. The next book published during the decade was Mrs. Susan Pollock's "National Kindergarten Manual." This was practical in character. The last one was Kate Douglas Wiggin's "Story of Patsy."

To make even a brief analysis of all the books that have appeared since 1890 would require more space than can be given here. The time of their appearance is of interest, and certain ones call for special consideration. The first book of the new decade was Miss Elizabeth Harrison's "Study of Child Nature," which was published in 1890.

The next was Bowen's "Froebel and Education by Self-activity," an English book published in the Great Educator Series in 1892. A volume of essays entitled "The Kindergarten," by Mrs. Wiggin and other prominent kindergartners, was published the same year, as was also the volume of essays called "Children's Rights," by Mrs. Wiggin and her sister, Nora A. Smith. Miss Jeannette R. Gregory's "Practical Suggestions to Kindergartners, Primary Teachers and Mothers" appeared in 1893, and Mrs. Mary C. Foster's "The Kindergarten of the Church" in 1894. The year 1895 was made memorable by the appearance of several books. One of these was Susan E. Blow's "Symbolic Education." Another was "Froebel's Mother Play Songs, A Commentary," by Denton J. Snider. A third was Mrs. Wiggin and Miss Smith's "Kindergarten Gifts," the first of the three volumes collectively termed "The Republic of Childhood." The second volume, "Kindergarten Occupations," and the third, "Kindergarten Principles and Practice," followed the next year. In 1896 Miss Katharine Beebe's "Home Occupations for Little Children" was published, and also Miss Frederica Beard's "Kindergarten Sunday School." In 1897 another book on the application of kindergarten principles to Sunday school work appeared, Miss Mabel Wilson's "Love, Light, and Life for God's Little Children." Mrs. Andrea Hofer Proudfoot also published "A Mother's Ideals," and Professor J. L. Hughes' "Froebel's Educational Laws for All Teachers." The volume called "Outlines for Kindergarten and Primary Classes," by Misses

Maud Cannell and Margaret E. Wise, was also published at about this time. Several additional books appeared in 1899. One of these was Miss Blow's "Letters to a Mother," another was Miss Emelie Poulsson's "Love and Law in Child Training," another was Miss Smith's "Kindergarten in a Nutshell," and still another was Frederick Burk's "Kindergarten Problem." The following year Mr. Snider's "Psychology of Froebel's Play Gifts" and Miss Harrison's "Two Children of the Foothills" were published, and also "The Message of Froebel" and "Children of the Future," by Miss Smith. Mr. Snider has since published the "Life of Froebel," and Miss Harrison "The Building Gifts" and "Some Silent Teachers."

Of the long list of books mentioned, all of which have served to further the kindergarten cause in some degree, a few call for special mention as indicating a special line of influence or illustrating a particular tendency. One of these is Miss Harrison's "Study of Child Nature," which has been translated into several languages, and is probably as widely known as any book on kindergarten subjects. This book was "the outcome of many years of experience in teaching young mothers to train their children in the home according to kindergarten principles," and although critics have declared it overdrawn, lacking in psychological value, and devoid of literary style, it meets the practical needs of the average mother better than many more pretentious books that have been written since its publication. The topics treated are such as appeal to mothers, and they are treated in a simple, practical manner. The chief value of the book, however, lies in the fact that it points out the advantage of building up the positive side of a child's nature. It has probably done as much as any one book on the list to acquaint mothers with kindergarten principles, and is an excellent one to awaken interest in the study of childhood.

Differing widely in content and literary merit, but similar in their appeal to the public outside of the teaching profession, are the books by Mrs. Kate Douglas Wiggin and Miss Nora A. Smith. These, too, were the outgrowth of experience, — "of talks and conferences on Froebel's educational principles with successive groups of earnest young women, here, there, and everywhere, for fifteen years." The purpose of the books was to acquaint the public with the kindergarten, its instrumentalities, — the gifts, games, songs, occupations, and stories, — and the method and purpose of their use. They were "purposely divested of technicalities and detail, in the hope that they would thus reach not only kindergarten students, but the many mothers and teachers who really long to know what Froebel's system of education is, and what it aims to do." These hopes have been more than realized. The public already familiar with "The Story of Patsy," and articles from the pen of its author, welcomed anything that the gifted sisters might produce, and the charming style in which the books are written made them welcome additions to any library. They have probably done more to popularize the kindergarten than have any other books written. They are of a kind that cannot grow old, and will continue their beneficent service to the cause of childhood for all time.

Quite different in its aim and scope, but far-reaching in its results, is the modest little book, "The Kindergarten Sunday-School," by Miss Beard. That the kindergarten had a message for the religious teachers of childhood had been recognized from the beginning, and the expression of Froebel's views concerning the child's spiritual nature, at Chautauqua and other gatherings, had led, as has been stated, to important changes in Sunday school method. But few of the many admirable things that had been said had got into book form, however, and Miss Beard's book was a real contribution to Sunday school literature. It contains a discussion of kindergarten principles in their application to Sunday school work, and outlines a series of lessons for a Sunday school kindergarten that deserves commendation because it is based on the children's power of comprehension, not upon a church calendar, nor upon a plan of lessons made out for adults. While Miss Beard might profitably have made her book larger, it has been of great value, and has had a great influence in establishing the principle, now generally recognized, that a pedagogical foundation is as essential in religious instruction as in any other.

While certain books were thus meeting the needs of certain classes of people, a book appeared that most admirably met the needs of school men, — whether or not they recognized that fact, — to many of whom the kinder-

garten still seems puerile, and Froebel without a message
to any save kindergartners. That book is Professor
Hughes's "Froebel's Educational Laws for all Teachers."
Since Froebel has been exploited mainly in connection
with the kindergarten, the educational public is inclined
to forget that he was the principal of a boys' school for
nearly twenty years before the idea of the kindergarten
even occurred to him, and that his educational views were
worked out with boys of varying ages before they were
applied to the education of little children at all. Mr.
Hughes says: "'The Education of Man' was written in
1826, fourteen years before he opened his first kindergarten, but if he had died in 1827 his contribution to
educational thought would have given him a foremost
place among educational reformers." Mr. Hughes emphasized the universal character of Froebel's principles,
and the effect of their application to grade work, in the
most admirable manner. The book is written from the
standpoint of a school man, for other school men, and it
has done much to bring about a more general recognition
of Froebel's principles.

Among the books claiming special attention is Miss
Blow's "Symbolic Education," in the estimation of many
the most noteworthy contribution to the literature of the
kindergarten since Froebel. To it one must go for the
philosophic interpretation of kindergarten principles and
practice. It is not a book to appeal to the superficial,
however, and its full significance will hardly dawn upon
even the most thoughtful, without careful study. It is

a book for the educational expert, and challenges the attention of the ablest thinkers. "It is one of the milestones in educational literature," says Miss Amalie Hofer in *The Kindergarten Magazine.* Miss Blow's later book, "Letters to a Mother," is along the same line, as are also the commentaries on Froebel by Denton J. Snider. They constitute an interpretation of Froebel, — an interpretation against which there is a growing reaction. For the philosophy of the eighteenth and early nineteenth centuries, which shaped to a large extent the theory and the practice of the kindergarten, has been replaced by a new interpretation of man and the universe, — the interpretation to which modern psychology gives the cue. The books in question present the theory of the kindergarten from the philosophical viewpoint most admirably, but that presentation is not one with which current educational thought is in sympathy.

As indicating the most extreme protest against the philosophical interpretation of the kindergarten, the unassuming little book by Frederick Burk, entitled "The Kindergarten Problem," is worthy of notice. While few kindergartners at the present time would be willing to cast kindergarten tradition aside to the extent that Mr. Burk has done, yet the book is stimulating and worthy of study, as an indication of the tendency that has been slowly coming to consciousness among the kindergartners of the country.

Resulting in part from the kindergarten movement is a group of books written mainly by mothers familiar with the new spirit in education and dealing principally with the problems of child training in the home. They are to be found in any list of books on child study, but differ from many of those classed under that head, since their aim is not merely the observation of facts in a child's development, but the application of the discovered principles of child training to the individual child in the individual home. The familiarity that most of these show with the child study movement as well as with other current educational movements is significant in showing the kind of motherhood the age is producing. Mr. John Brisben Walker considers that one of the six distinct lines in which women have progressed since the Chicago Exposition is "the acceptance of motherhood as a profession." The books in question are proof that motherhood is being so considered. The books of this character were later in appearing than those on the kindergarten as such, but by their insight into its purposes and the tacit approval of its principles they have been of great value in furthering the kindergarten movement.

Among them are the following: "Children, their Models and Critics," by Mrs. Aldrich, published in 1892; "Beckonings from Little Hands," by Patterson Du Bois, 1894; "Child Culture in the Home," by Mrs. Martha Mosher, and "The Study of a Child" by Mrs. Louise Hogan, both of which appeared in 1898; "Nursery Ethics" and "From the Child's Standpoint," by Mrs. Florence Hull Winterburn, published in 1899; "Concerning Children," by Mrs. Charlotte Perkins Gilman, and "Childhood" by

Mrs. Theodore W. Birney, published in 1900; Grinnell's "How John and I Brought up the Child" and Chenery's "As the Twig is Bent" also belong to this class, as do several of the books by kindergartners already named, — particularly Miss Blow's "Letters to a Mother," Miss Smith's "Children of the Future," Mrs. Proudfoot's "A Mother's Ideals," and Miss Harrison's "A Study of Child Nature." Since these were not inspired by the kindergarten movement, and cannot be considered its product, no mention is made of a long list of books on child study and genetic psychology as such, whose purpose is scientific observation. Most of these, however, have reënforced the fundamental conclusions concerning childhood which underlie kindergarten procedure, and have therefore served an excellent purpose in advancing the kindergarten cause.

The increasing influence of the kindergarten was not due wholly to the increasing literature of the kind mentioned. The appreciation of the kindergarten for school purposes came rather through practical than through theoretical lines. The things which the kindergarten had emphasized at first, — the gifts and occupations, — had appealed to the primary teacher mainly as means of busy work. But when the story began to claim a larger place, when gardening and nature excursions became a part of the kindergarten program, and when the child's song began to receive increasing attention, she began to wake up. The kindergarten song book contained songs of a quality not to be found in the primary school repertoire. The stories designed for kindergarten use appealed to the children's interest as her own, if she had any, did not. Why should the kindergarten song or story book be confined to kindergarten use alone? Until the kindergarten came, the rote song was almost unknown in school work. The story, too, was barely recognized as an educational instrument. There may have been a carefully graded course in music, but the children were drilled in the elements of musical notation, and seldom sang the songs that they really loved. There were courses in reading and language, but little or no telling of the stories dear to the heart of every child. Children were taught to read, write, and spell, but were given no food for the imagination.

The need of new and better songs, and of more and better stories for kindergarten use, had made itself felt in the early years of the movement. When that need was supplied for the kindergarten, it was supplied in large measure for the primary school as well. Perhaps none of the kindergarten instrumentalities has received a greater measure of criticism than the songs originally devised for kindergarten use. Without denying the value of song in connection with the gift plays, it must be admitted that the conditions for true musical feeling and real musical expression are lacking in most of these. The composition of songs truly musical and childlike in thought, word, and melody was one of the tasks to be accomplished if the kindergarten was to further the child's musical development to the degree that it should. That this was recognized is shown by the large number of kindergarten song books that have been published since 1880. The first of these in

order of time was Clara Beeson Hubbard's "Merry Songs
and Games," published in 1881. Next came Mrs. Wiggin's "Kindergarten Chimes," published in 1885. Miss
Eleanor Smith's "Songs for Little Children" and Mrs.
Hailman's "Songs, Games, and Rhymes" for kindergarten
and primary school appeared in 1887. These seemed to
meet the demand for a few years, and then came "Stories
in Song," by Misses Emerson and Brown, in 1890. "Songs
and Games for Little Ones," by Misses Jenks and Walker,
in 1892, and "Song Stories for the Kindergarten," by
Misses Patty and Mildred Hill, in 1893. From 1896 on
several others appeared. Among these are: "Song
Echoes," by the Misses Jenks and Rust; "Small Songs
for Small Singers," by Professor Neidlinger; "Songs for
the Child World," by Mrs. Jessie L. Gaynor, and "Holiday
Songs," compiled by Miss Emelie Poulsson. Miss Clara
L. Anderson's "Instrumental Characteristic Rhythms"
and Miss Mari Ruef Hofer's "Music for the Child World"
have met an additional musical need of the kindergarten,
— that for appropriate marches and other forms of instrumental music. They have furnished a stimulus to
musical interpretation on the part of children, and have
given the kindergartner's musical repertoire a richness that
it did not have in the earlier years. By the publication of
her two books on traditional games, the one entitled
"Singing Games," published in 1896, and the other,
"Popular Folk Games," published in 1907, Miss Hofer
has rendered the kindergarten an additional service.
The customary kindergarten games had been criticised

as being too largely symbolical and lacking in the elements that constitute a good game. The application of the kindergarten idea to school and playground showed the need of games of a different kind, and the books in question are a response to that need. Although many of the games are intended for children beyond the kindergarten age, the spirit of the books has brought about a new attitude toward the games of the kindergarten proper, — an attitude that promises well for the future.

Considering the recognition given to the child's love of rhyme and story, it is somewhat surprising that the kindergarten story book should have been nearly a decade later than the song book in making its appearance. Miss Poulsson had published her "Finger Rhymes" in 1889, but no story books appeared until the following year. During the year no less than four appeared, — Miss Sara E. Wiltse's "Kindergarten Stories and Morning Talks"; Mrs. Van Kirk's "Stories for the Kindergarten and Home"; "The Story Hour" by Mrs. Wiggin and Miss Smith; and "Kindergarten Gems" by Misses Ketchum and Jorgenson. Others soon followed—"Child's Christ Tales" and Miss Wiltse's "Stories for Kindergarten and Primary School" in 1892, the "Boston Collection of Kindergarten Stories," Miss Poulsson's collection entitled, "In the Child's World," and Miss Howliston's "Cat Tails and Other Tales" in 1893. The last-named book was not distinctively a kindergarten collection, though it belongs to the kindergarten story books in spirit. Miss Harrison's "In Story Land" appeared in 1895, and since

N

that date a number of others have been published. Among these are Mrs. Clara Dillingham Pierson's collections of animal stories, — "Among the Meadow People," "Among the Farmyard People," etc., Miss Madge Bigham's "Stories of Mother Goose Village," and Miss Maud Lindsay's "Mother Stories." The number of good collections of stories for use in the primary grades has become too large to mention.

The publication of the above-named story books, particularly the earlier ones, had a special value at the time of their appearance, in the early nineties. The story has come to hold an important place as an educational instrument in the primary grades, but as before stated, its use was but beginning at the time in question. The kindergarten story has been peculiarly the vehicle of the kindergarten thought, and has come to have definite and easily recognized earmarks of its own. The fact that there were practically no other collections of stories in the educational market at the time gave the kindergarten story books a special value, and obtained for them a large use among primary teachers. The service that the kindergarten song book rendered in acquainting primary teachers with the kindergarten principles has been mentioned, but the service that the collections of kindergarten stories rendered was no less marked.

No record of kindergarten literature during the period under consideration would be complete that did not include a mention of the kindergarten periodicals, — *The Kindergarten Magazine, The Kindergarten Review*, and *The*

Child Garden. The story of *The Kindergarten Messenger*, and of *The New Education* has been told in an earlier chapter. When the latter became merged in *The Public School* of Boston in 1883, the kindergarten movement was left without representation in the field of educational journalism, and remained so until 1888 when *The Kindergarten Magazine* was founded by Mrs. Alice B. and Miss Cora L. Stockham of Chicago. The new magazine was carried on under their management until August, 1892, when it was purchased by Miss Amalie Hofer and Miss Andrea Hofer, now Mrs. Proudfoot. The following year it became the organ of the Kindergarten Literature Company, a stock company that had been organized by a number of the leading kindergartners of the country for the promotion of the kindergarten cause. Miss Amalie Hofer retained the editorship of *The Kindergarten Magazine* and Miss Andrea Hofer assumed the responsibility of *The Child Garden*, a new magazine of story song and play, established in 1892 and published by the same company. This magazine did excellent service in furnishing stories and suggestions during the ten or more years of existence, but it was finally discontinued. *The Kindergarten Magazine* continued under the able leadership of Miss Amalie Hofer until 1903, when it was transferred to Miss Bertha Johnston and Miss Minerva Jourdan. In 1906 it became the property of Dr. E. Lyell Earle of New York City. It is now *The Kindergarten and Primary Magazine*.

The Kindergarten Review, which for the past nine years

has shared the field of kindergarten journalism with *The Kindergarten Magazine*, began its existence as *The Kindergarten News* in Buffalo in 1890. It was edited by Louis H. Allen and published as the organ of the Buffalo Free Kindergarten Association. It eventually became the property of the Milton Bradley Company of Springfield, Mass., and was ably edited by Henry W. Blake. When the Misses Emelie and Laura Poulsson succeeded to the editorship upon Mr. Blake's death in 1897, the publication was enlarged and its name changed to *The Kindergarten Review*. The Misses Poulsson continued the editorship until 1904, when it was assumed by Miss May Murray, who still conducts it.

It would be well-nigh impossible to estimate the value of the service that these publications have rendered the kindergarten and the cause of American education in general. *The Kindergarten Magazine* appeared when the movement was still largely unorganized, and public opinion on the subject was still in the process of formation.

During the important period from 1890 to 1900, when the movement was spreading out and assuming definite character, the editor traveled at her own expense, organizing kindergartens, associations, and training schools, following up every symptom of interest that manifested itself. A similar service was rendered by Mrs. Lucretia Willard Treat. By reports of the work in the different kindergarten centers, by accounts of meetings of interest to kindergartners, and by articles along kindergarten and allied lines, *The Kindergarten Magazine* gave unity to the movement and served as a watch tower from which the field of kindergarten progress could be scanned. The splendid enthusiasm shown by the kindergartners of the country at the time of the Columbian Exposition was augmented by and reflected in *The Kindergarten Magazine*, and the success which the kindergarten scored on that occasion was due in no small degree to its efforts. From 1888 to 1901 not less than two thousand articles on the kindergarten and allied phases of elementary education, written by the ablest educators of the country, had appeared in its pages. By its practical suggestions no less than by its reports from the kindergarten field, it has translated the kindergarten ideal into actual kindergarten procedure, not only to young kindergartners but to mothers and educators all over the land. It has had a positive tone, moreover, and has spoken in no uncertain voice on questions of educational policy. It has reflected the social movement and has interpreted educational progress anew, in terms of the great West. It has furthered the kindergarten cause in a material way, — the Kindergarten Literature Company having, during a particular period of four years, earned and spent $10,000 in sending out literature and establishing kindergartens.

The Kindergarten Review came into the field later, when much of the pioneer work had been done, but it has rendered a like service during the years of its existence. The bound volumes of these publications are indispensable to any one wishing to gain an insight into the origin and growth of the kindergarten movement in the United States.

The literature of the kindergarten, both periodical and permanent, has won a place for itself in American life and thought. The library of the teacher is incomplete without an infusion of Froebelian doctrine; the church worker unfamiliar with it is out of touch with current problems; the home that has not felt its influence lacks some of the qualities the ideal home possesses. Horace Scudder says that the literature of the world has been greatly enriched since poverty and childhood have been annexed to its domain. The educational literature of America has been greatly enriched by the contribution of the kindergarten; the kindergarten, the kindergarten child, and the kindergartner herself have gained entrance to the field of general literature, there to do service in the cause of human advancement.

CHAPTER X

THE KINDERGARTEN IN THE PUBLIC SCHOOL SYSTEM

THAT the kindergarten had been well recommended by means of the agencies described in preceding chapters cannot be questioned, and its speedy adoption by the school was anticipated by the oversanguine. During the first decade of the period under consideration such adoption was far from being as rapid as some had hoped, however, although this was not wholly an unmixed evil. The reasons for such tardiness were not far to seek. The kindergarten associations were only beginning their work and required time to make their influence felt. The other agencies that have aided in building up sentiment favorable to the kindergarten either did not come into existence until the decade between 1880 and 1890 or were not strong enough to exert the influence which they exercised later. The church needed a deeper insight into the social significance of Christianity before it could advocate the kindergarten with vigor. The Woman's Christian Temperance Union, organized in 1874, did not undertake work bearing upon the kindergarten until nearly the middle of the next decade. Women's clubs, the first of which was organized in 1878, did not undertake the study of education until many years later. The first social settlement in the

United States was not opened until 1887, and the study of education in universities and colleges had hardly more than begun. The "new psychology" did not make itself felt until the latter part of the decade under consideration, and the new conception of education did not become sufficiently general to be dynamic until the decade following. While a sufficient number of cities became converted to kindergarten adoption during this decade to prove that the kindergarten was making itself felt, it was not until the last decade of the century that public school kindergartens became common. If there is any appropriateness in calling the decade from 1880 to 1890 the Association Decade in kindergarten history, the decade from 1890 to 1900 may with equal appropriateness be called the Public School Decade in the kindergarten movement. Kindergarten associations had been formed before 1880, it is true, and their organization did not cease with the close of the decade. So, too, public school kindergartens had come into existence before 1890, and their number is rapidly increasing, although that decade has passed. Each became general, however, during the decade named. The adoption of the kindergarten before 1890 was infrequent enough to occasion comment when it occurred. The non-adoption of that institution is likely to occasion comment at the present time.

Apart from these general considerations, the main reasons for the slow march of kindergarten progress were two. One was the expense of maintaining kindergartens, which was supposed to be much greater than that of maintaining primary schools. This is due in part to the cost of kindergarten material, but in greater measure to the larger number of teachers supposed to be required for a given number of children. "The surprises of experiences," to use Miss Blow's apt phrase, have corrected this impression. Her own words on this point are of interest. "In the early days of the kindergarten movement we were told over and over again that the Froebelian ideal could not be carried out if there were more than ten or fifteen children in a kindergarten. A kindergarten of fifty was condemned by the intolerant as a surrender to the hostile powers, and was excused by the tolerant as perhaps an unavoidable bowing in the house of Rimmon. To-day I do not hesitate in saying that as far as my observation goes, the average educational results reached in the larger kindergartens far surpass the average results reached in a kindergarten attended by ten or fifteen children." The bugbear of expense continued to frighten school boards for many years, however, and the objection continues to be raised even now. In 1886 the Commissioner of Education said: "The work of making the kindergarten a part of the school system is only a question of time. The most eminent educators of the day recognize and indorse its principles and methods, but the expense involved prevents its becoming at once the lowest grade of the public school system." Superintendent Seaver of Boston said at about the same time, "The next step forward is to recognize and establish the kindergarten as a part of the system of public instruction."

In spite of the slowness of its adoption by the school, however, the kindergarten was making itself felt, even in those communities that never adopted it as such. Kindergarten song books found their way to primary teachers' desks; plants and pictures appeared in schoolroom windows and on schoolroom walls; and the presence of scissors, folding papers, sewing cards, and modeling clay was pointed to as evidence that "the kindergarten was being introduced." School boards and superintendents were delighted to have the primary teachers assume the kindergarten manner, and learn something of "kindergarten methods." "Little progress has been made in the establishment of kindergartens at public expense," said Dr. Harris towards the end of the decade, "nevertheless the system has had a marked effect in improving the methods in the primary grades." But while many cities thus dabbled in the edges of the kindergarten pool or stood hesitating upon its brink, but few had the courage to take the real plunge. To many the adoption of "kindergarten methods" in the school rather than the adoption of the kindergarten itself seemed quite sufficient. The interest awakened by the kindergarten as a part of the school system, which had made St. Louis the center of educational interest during the seventies, seemed transferred to an interest in the adoption of the characteristic features of the kindergarten in the grades. During the eighties, therefore, educational interest was transferred from St. Louis to La Porte, Ind., and the Cook County Normal School in Chicago, where Professor W. N. Hailman and Colonel Francis W. Parker were respectively engaged in the attempt to pour the wine of the new educational thought into the bottles of traditional school conditions.

The second reason for the slowness of kindergarten adoption by the school was more fundamental. The school laws of most states did not permit of the expenditure of public school funds for the education of children of kindergarten age. But three states in the Union have a school age of four years, — Connecticut, Wisconsin, and Oregon. These are, therefore, the only states in which children of kindergarten age can be educated at public expense. Whether kindergarten work may legally be substituted for the customary grade work without legislative action depends upon the school law of the individual states. In two states, Massachusetts and Rhode Island, there is no age limit for entering school. In these states, therefore, the school age furnished no obstacle to the establishment of kindergartens. In eleven additional states — Maine, New Hampshire, Vermont, New York, New Jersey, Mississippi, Michigan, Minnesota, Iowa, Kansas, Nebraska, and the territory of New Mexico — the school age is five years. Children entering school at the age of five are still within the period for which the kindergarten is intended. Whether kindergarten work may be substituted for the customary grade work during the first year depends in these states also upon the school law of the individual states. In Maine, New Hampshire, Kansas, and Nebraska the law allows the local school authorities to determine the character of the school instruction. If they see fit to substitute kindergarten for the customary first-grade instruction, there is nothing in the law to prevent their doing so. Unless the admission of children below the legal age is desired, therefore, no legislation is needed in these states to make the kindergarten a part of the school system. This is also true in Nevada and South Dakota, in which the school age is six. In the other states of the group in question legislation was necessary before kindergartens could be legally established.

In the states in which the school age is six or more the problem is somewhat different. In Alabama and Virginia the school age is seven; in Texas it is eight. In all the other states not already mentioned, it is six. That six-year-old children can still be benefited by attending kindergarten, no one will question. The kindergarten was primarily intended, however, for children below that age, and school authorities may well question the advisability of spending public school money for kindergartens for children of six years. If the children are to gain the real benefit that the kindergarten is intended to confer, a lowering of the school age is needed in states of this class. A general lowering of the school age in a given state, for the sake of making the establishment of kindergartens possible, must of necessity impose a hardship, however, upon the localities where kindergartens cannot be established. The legislation to make the establishment of kindergartens possible in states of this class has usually specified that children below the legal age should be admitted in case of the establishment of kindergartens only. Several of the states in question have enacted such legislation. Others have attempted it without success, and some consider that the time to effect it has not yet come. Missouri, the first state to establish public kindergartens, has a school age of six years. When the initial experiment with the kindergarten was made in St. Louis, children of five years were admitted, but the legal age of entrance has since been insisted upon, and the children in the St. Louis kindergartens, as well as those in the kindergartens of Kansas City, are all, therefore, six or more years of age. The attempt to lower the school age has been made several times without success. The children who attended the first kindergartens in New Orleans were six likewise, but the age at which children might be admitted to kindergartens was lowered by the Constitutional Convention of 1898. In several of the Southern states that have adopted the kindergarten the children are of legal age, — six or more. These facts are mentioned to show the difficulties with which the kindergarten had to contend in becoming a part of the school system. In general, "any city, through powers inherent in its charter, may maintain kindergartens provided they are supported wholly by local taxation." During the decade from 1880 to 1890, as far as known, but three states enacted legislation to make the establishment of kindergartens possible. These were Vermont, Indiana, and Connecticut. Cities in other states that adopted the kindergarten during this decade did so through powers inherent in their charters, or because legislation was unnecessary.

In spite of the difficulties still to be surmounted, the kindergarten made its way into the school from 1880 to 1890 with a fair degree of success. Boston had established a public school kindergarten in 1870, which was, however, discontinued after a few years of existence. The organization of the St. Louis kindergartens had been effected in 1873, as has been stated. No records can be found to show that it was adopted by any other public school during the decade from 1870 to 1880 with the exception of Forestville, Ill., a suburb of Chicago and now a part of the city. This was for many years the only public school kindergarten in Illinois. The cities to adopt it during the decade from 1880 to 1890 were as follows: Milwaukee, Wis., in 1881; Fort Collins, Colo., in 1882; Des Moines, Ia., and Portland, Me., in 1883; Muskegon, Mich., and La Porte, Ind., in 1884; New Orleans, La., Hartford, Conn., and Sheboygan, Wis., in 1886; Boston, Mass., and Philadelphia, Pa., in 1887; Rochester, N.Y., in 1888; Los Angeles, Cal., in 1889. Several other cities are known to have adopted public school kindergartens during the decade, but the exact date could not be determined. Among these are: Burlington, Bayfield, Baraboo, Lake Geneva, and Hayward, Wis.; New Rochelle, Mt. Vernon, White Plains, Yonkers, Port Chester, and Carlstadt, N.Y.; Grand Rapids and Ann Arbor, Mich.; Providence and Newport, R.I.; and Pueblo, Colo. This is a fair showing, since it included five of the larger cities of the country, — St. Louis, Milwaukee, Boston, Philadelphia, and New Orleans. Each of these cities was a center whose influence could not fail to be widely felt. It must not be supposed, however, that a complete system of kindergartens was established at one stroke in the cities in question. In Philadelphia the thirty kindergartens that had been established and maintained by the Sub-Primary School Society were assumed by the board of education, and in Boston the fourteen that had been established and maintained by Mrs. Shaw. In Los Angeles twelve kindergartens were adopted by the school, but in most cases the experiment was made with one or two, and additional ones were opened as these first ones proved successful.

The acceptance of the kindergarten as a part of the school system during the decade in question was both indicated and advanced by the organization of kindergarten departments in state and city normal schools. Such departments had been created in the state normal schools at Oshkosh, Wis., and Winona, Minn., in 1880. In 1882 they were added to the normal schools at Oswego and Fredonia in New York, and at Emporia, Kan. Connecticut added such departments to its normal schools at about the same time, and Michigan did the same in 1889. Other schools may have taken the same action, but the date of the establishment of the kindergarten departments could not be ascertained. The training of kindergartners has not been the chief aim of these departments; in fact some of them make no effort in that direction. They aim in large part to acquaint the students in the general courses with the procedure of the kindergarten and the principles upon which such procedure is based, as a matter of educational intelligence. Though not a state institution, the Cook County Normal School, established in 1883, must be included because of its wide influence in this direction, under the leadership of Colonel Parker. A similar influence is exerted by those city normal schools having a general course but including a kindergarten department. Of these, such institutions as the Philadelphia Normal School and the Boston Normal School are conspicuous examples. "It is through the normal school that the adjustment of Froebel's system to our public schools must be made, if it is to be made at all," said Commissioner Harris in 1884, commenting on the recent establishment of kindergarten departments in such schools. That they have exerted a marked influence on the spread of Froebelian thought is generally recognized. That they will compel the reorganization of existing forms of kindergarten training in the near future is evident to those who have made a study of the matter.

At the beginning of the last decade of the century the kindergarten outlook was fairly promising, although the clear-sighted realized that much effort was still needed to place it upon the proper basis as a part of the educational system. In the cities where the kindergarten had been adopted it was winning golden opinions, and the results were more than justifying the hopes of its friends. At the Toronto meeting of the N. E. A. in 1891 the following resolutions were passed : "Resolved that we view with pleasure the spread of kindergarten principles and methods and trust that they may be generally introduced into the public schools. To this end we recommend that the different states secure the necessary legislation that will enable communities to support and maintain kindergartens at public expense." Such legislation was one of the features of kindergarten progress during the decade then just entered upon.

The effort that the kindergartners of the country felt it necessary to make for their cause at the Columbian Exposition and the organization and unification of the kindergarten forces that such effort demanded, have been discussed in another chapter. The kindergarten cause would have continued to advance had there been no such event, but ten years of effort without it could hardly have accomplished as much as was accomplished by its means. Nothing short of an occasion so momentous could have brought the kindergartners from all parts of the country together and nothing less than an opportunity so great could have spurred them on to the effort made. The indorsement and influence of the exposition leaders and managers; the legislation enacted within the next few years; the books written, and the extension of the kindergarten into new circles of influence, — all these combined to make the last decade of the century a memorable one in kindergarten history.

It would be impossible to enumerate even the principal cities that adopted the kindergarten during the decade under consideration, but the fact that nearly all the larger cities did so is significant. Though several strategic cities adopted it before the Columbian Exposition, the

o

larger number that did so during the latter part of the decade is a proof of the increasing momentum occasioned by that event. Among those adopting it the first few years of the decade were the following: in 1891, Racine and Dodgeville, Wis., Lexington, Ky., Utica, N.Y., Saginaw, Mich., San Jose, Cal., and Sun Dance, Wyo., the latter being the first public school kindergarten to be established in the state; in 1892, St. Paul, Minn., Chicago and Evanston, Ill., Beloit and Superior, Wis., San Diego, Cal., Worcester, Mass., and Cohoes, N.Y.; in 1893, New York City, Syracuse, and Jamestown, N.Y., Omaha and Lincoln, Neb., and El Paso, Texas, — the first one to be established in that state. During the latter half of the decade the kindergarten gained entrance into the following cities: Sacramento, Cal., Denver, Col., Newark, N.J., Cleveland and Dayton, Ohio, Kansas City, Mo., Council Bluffs, Ia., Portland, Ore., Washington, D.C., Louisville, Ky., Spokane, Wash., Buffalo, N.Y., and doubtless several others. Kindergartens are conducted in seventy or more public schools in Pittsburg and Allegheny, but they are controlled by the Pittsburg and Allegheny Kindergarten Associations, though the school boards of the two cities contribute generously to their support. In the Report of the Commissioner of Education for 1897–1898, one hundred eighty-nine cities of over eight thousand inhabitants are named as maintaining public kindergartens. There are doubtless as many smaller ones doing the same. The number of kindergartens given for these one hundred eighty-nine cities was thirteen hundred sixty-five, a number known to be much too small. Dr. Harris states that the most difficult statistical work of the Bureau for 1897 and 1898 and the most unsatisfactory in its results was that of collecting information concerning the kindergartens. The proportion of public school kindergartens sending returns was doubtless greater than the proportion of private ones. Of the three thousand of the latter known to be in existence nearly one half failed to reply to the request for information. Unsatisfactory as the data are, they form some basis for computing the entire number of kindergartens in the country, public, private, and charitable. By the end of the century, five thousand would be a conservative estimate. In 1903 Miss Anderson's Annual, already referred to, gave a list of over four hundred forty cities maintaining public kindergartens. The discrepancy between these figures and those given by the Bureau of Education is due in part probably to the increase during the five years that had passed, but more to the other fact that all the cities and towns were given, regardless of their size. According to this the five states having the largest number of cities in which public school kindergartens have been adopted are: New York, 86; Wisconsin, 71; New Jersey, 56; Michigan, 43; Massachusetts, 34. The increase since the new century opened has been most gratifying, and includes several of the larger cities that had not hitherto adopted them. Among these are Minneapolis, Baltimore, Buffalo, Toledo, Cincinnati, and Detroit, in the order named.

The progress of the kindergarten in the South since the

opening of the new century has been particularly gratifying. Of the 189 cities mentioned by the Commissioner of Education as maintaining kindergartens in 1897–1898, 94 were in the North Atlantic group; but 2 in the Southern Atlantic; 8 in the South Central; 68 in the North Central; and 17 in the Western. In an article prepared by Miss Eveline A. Waldo of New Orleans for the St. Louis meeting of the N. E. A. in 1904, it is stated that public school kindergartens have been established in all the Southern states but four, — South Carolina, Florida, Tennessee, and Arkansas. The conclusion that there were none in these states was based upon the fact that the persons questioned had not replied to her inquiry. In addition to these four, Miss Anderson's Annual indicates that in 1903, at least, there were none in Idaho, Delaware, North Dakota, South Dakota, and West Virginia, — a total of nine. In 1907 public school kindergartens had been established in West Virginia also.

The kindergarten is becoming a part of the school system also in the countries that have recently come under the control of the United States. It forms an integral part of the school system of Cuba, it has secured a foothold in Porto Rico, and is making rapid progress in the Philippines. The report of the Secretary of Public Instruction of the Philippine Islands for 1904 speaks of the kindergartens of Manila in the following words: "This work has been rapidly developed in the past year. Seven kindergartens are maintained, one being for English-speaking children. Seven American teachers are engaged in the work in Manila under the direction of a highly qualified supervisor. There are twelve Filipino assistants. The attendance has been good and the interest excellent. In many cases there have been applications for membership far exceeding the capacity of the schools. Mothers' meetings have been held with exhibits of the work of the children, and these seem to have been enthusiastically received, the attendance often running as high as fifty.

"As stated above, the work has as one of its objects the training of young women to give kindergarten instruction in the provinces. The desire is to have a successful kindergarten established in each provincial capital, not only for its value to the children attending, but also as an exhibit to the public of correct teaching principles, and as a feature of the training of the primary teacher."

The legislation which has enabled the kindergarten to become a part of the school system to this extent is worthy of attention. As already stated, Vermont, Indiana, and Connecticut secured the legislation needed to make kindergartens possible in 1888. The first state to legislate upon the subject during the decade between 1890 and 1900 was Michigan, which in 1891 passed a law authorizing the establishment of kindergartens for children between the ages of four and seven years. The next state to take action was Ohio, which in 1893 secured the passage of a bill authorizing the establishment of kindergartens for children between four and six years of age, but providing that they must be supported wholly by local taxation. Although bills providing for the establishment of kindergartens had been presented to two preceding legislatures, Illinois did not secure the passage of a bill to that effect until 1895. Kindergartens had been opened in Chicago, although there was no legal sanction for this action. The bill referred to provided for the support of the kindergartens, not from the school tax fund of the state, but from the local fund. This meant that the kindergarten must be submitted to the vote of the people. It was not so submitted, however, until 1899, when unforeseen circumstances made it inevitable. A shortage of the school funds threatened the abolishing of the sixty-three kindergartens that had been established, and the kindergarten was therefore submitted to the people at the spring election. The 87,000 votes cast in its favor to the 15,000 cast against it placed the kindergarten upon a secure footing in that city from that time on.

The stimulus given to the kindergarten movement by the Chicago Exposition is shown in part by the number of states that passed laws before the decade closed, making the establishment of public school kindergartens possible. These were Washington, New York, Pennsylvania, Iowa, Wisconsin, California, Oregon, Colorado, Louisiana, Minnesota, Montana, New Jersey, the District of Columbia, and the territory of Arizona. Several others, Virginia, Oklahoma, Florida, Texas, Utah, and Idaho, have enacted laws to the same effect since the new century opened. Laws authorizing the establishment of public school kindergartens have also been passed in West Virginia, Maryland, and Wyoming, but the date of the legislation in question could not be learned. Since Maine, New Hampshire, Kansas, Nebraska, South Dakota, and Nevada consider that kindergartens may be established without legislation to that effect, and legislation is unnecessary in Massachusetts and Rhode Island because the schools are supported almost wholly by local taxation, it appears that the kindergarten has a legal foothold in all but eleven states. These are Delaware, North Carolina, South Carolina, Georgia, Alabama, Mississippi, Arkansas, Kentucky, Tennessee, Missouri, and North Dakota.

The momentum which the kindergarten gained in the last decade of the century is indicated in part by the increased number of state normal schools which added kindergarten departments during that period. Although the exact number cannot be determined, it is known that a large number did so. Among these were Bridgewater and North Adams among the Massachusetts normal schools; the Providence Normal School in Rhode Island; Albany, Buffalo, Plattsburg, and Cortland, among the normal schools of New York; Slippery Rock and California among those of Pennsylvania; Mt. Pleasant and Marquette among these of Michigan; Chico, Los Angeles, and San Jose, among those of California; Greely, in Colorado; St. Cloud and Mankato among those in Minnesota; Milwaukee and River Falls in Wisconsin; and those at Trenton, New Jersey, Peru, Nebraska, and Salt Lake City, Utah. Kindergarten departments have since been added to the normal schools at Normal, Ill.; at Cedar Falls, Iowa; at Natchitoches, La.; at Kalamazoo,

Mich.; at Duluth, Minn.; at Kirksville, Mo.; at Lock Haven, Pa.; at Farmville, Va.; Stevens Point and Superior, Wis.; and at the three newly established normal schools in Oklahoma. This list, known to be incomplete, included twenty-one states and not less than fifty institutions. What may not be hoped for from the influence of these institutions for the cause of the kindergarten and of educational progress? The kindergartners belonging to this class show an energy and an alertness as one meets them at I. K. U. gatherings, that testifies to their influence in their own localities, and promises much for the future of kindergarten training. Most of them are relatively young, and have not yet gained a national reputation, but from among them will come some of the future leaders of the movement.

The student of kindergarten history cannot fail to be impressed by the increasing number of institutions for higher education, not supported by state funds, that are adding kindergarten departments. While the claim to the title of college or university may be somewhat doubtful in the case of a few, the list of such institutions given by Miss Anderson contains several of national reputation. It is as follows: Winthrop Normal and Industrial College, Rock Hill, S.C.; Stetson University, Deland, Fla.; Drake University, Des Moines, Ia.; Friends University, Wichita, Kansas, and Campbell University, Holton, Kansas; Kee Mar College, Hagarstown, Md.; Alma College, Alma, Mich.; Wesleyan University, Lincoln, Nebraska; Adelphi College, and Pratt Institute, Brooklyn, N.Y.; Columbia

University, N.Y.; the University of Chicago; Latter
Day Saints University, Salt Lake City, Utah; Stout
Manual Training School, Menomonie, Wis.; Epworth
University, Oklahoma City, Okla.; Valparaiso College
and Northern Indiana Normal School, Valparaiso, Ind.;
and Temple College, Philadelphia, Pa.

In addition to the departments for kindergarten training in these institutions and in the state normal schools
already mentioned, there are not less than one hundred
training schools that are either private or supported by
cities or associations. This increase in the number of
training schools, and the growing necessity for kindergarten supervision in the larger cities, has given rise to a
new need in the kindergarten world, — the need for
adequate training for the kindergarten training teachers
and supervisors. This need is being admirably met at
the present time at Teachers College. The courses of
instruction offered by this institution are such as to acquaint the would-be leader with the theory and practice
of the kindergarten in its relation to the whole of education, and to familiarize her with the larger problems of
kindergarten training and supervision.

The growing appreciation of the kindergarten as a part
of the state educational system was further shown during
the last decade of the century by the establishment of
kindergartens in state homes for dependent and neglected
children, and in institutions for the defective classes —
the blind, deaf, and feeble-minded. A beginning had
been made in that direction before 1890, but a beginning

only. The story of dependent and neglected childhood and its care and education is both sad and long. There are in the United States at the present time over six hundred institutions, public and private, for such children, which in 1890 enrolled 65,000 children. How many of these were of kindergarten age no one can tell, but doubtless a goodly number. State provision has been made in a number of instances, either in the form of state homes, county homes, or support in private homes or institutions. When such institutions are near public schools the older children attend these, but the children of kindergarten age cannot easily do so unless the distance is short. The need of a kindergarten in the building thus becomes apparent. Eleven states have made provision for homeless children in state homes, and three in county homes, and in a number of these kindergartens have been established. The first of the state homes to be built was that at Coldwater, Michigan, in 1885. Minnesota, Wisconsin, and Rhode Island made a similar provision the same year, and Kansas, Colorado, and Texas did so soon after. The other states having such institutions are Nebraska, Montana, Nevada, and Iowa. A kindergarten was connected with the Michigan institution almost from the beginning, and with the institutions in Wisconsin and Minnesota soon after their opening. No statistics concerning the number of kindergartens in such homes have ever been gathered. Miss Anderson gives but twenty, though this is known to be far too small. The excellent results obtained in the institutions where kindergartens have been adopted cannot but increase their number in the near future.

The value of the kindergarten for defective children had been realized before the last decade of the century, but its general introduction into institutions for the deaf, blind, and feeble-minded belongs to the decade in question. Such introduction is interwoven with the history of the efforts to instruct these different classes of defectives. In the earlier years children were not admitted to the schools for the deaf until the period for which the kindergarten is intended was over. When this age was lowered, as it has been in recent years, the kindergarten began to be considered, and according to Mr. Edward E. Allen, in Butler's "Education in the United States," "kindergarten methods have been made use of more and more, although no true kindergarten can be conducted in schools where language comes so late and so hard, where even natural signs are arbitrarily interdicted, and where there can be no music. But the occupations and games are widely applicable, and are universally used." In 1901 there were one hundred eighteen institutions for teaching the deaf, according to Dexter's "History of Education in the United States." Of the fifty-seven state institutions, thirty had kindergartens. With the tendency to substitute oral instruction for instruction in the sign language, and day schools for the large institutions, the kindergarten will become still more general. Now that kindergarten departments have been added to so many institutions pupils are urged to enter at an earlier age.

In the institutions for the blind also, the kindergarten has added much to the children's enjoyment and profit.

Here, too, the age at which children are admitted has been lowered in recent years. Hence kindergartens have been established, and they are proving of the greatest benefit. On this point Mr. Allen says: "Children with good sight and hearing have got along without kindergarten training and so have blind children, but of all the useful means of reaching and developing the average blind child, none is so effective as a properly conducted kindergarten. It is not easy to overestimate the importance of hearing in giving children language and all that this means; song and the joy it brings and the deep feeling it inspires. The practical knowledge of things comes to the blind through the hand, their fingers being veritable projections of the brain. Thus must not only their hands be trained to sensitiveness of touch, but to be strong and supple, so that they may indeed be dextrous; for as their hands are, so are their brains. The kindergarten cultivates ear and heart and hand and brain as nothing else does. Even color is not wholly omitted. Kindergartens for the blind may be true kindergartens in every sense of the word. A kindergartner of fully sensed children would miss only the brightness coming from the untrammeled ability to run and play and the absence of all that sight brings. The kindergartens for the blind have as their end and aim this very rousing of children, and the putting them in touch with their surroundings." As Mr. Allen is superintendent of the Pennsylvania State Institution for the Blind, he knows whereof he speaks. How many of the thirty-nine institutions for the blind have kindergartens could not be ascertained. Mr. Dexter says that "the kindergarten is an almost universal part of such institutions and that no other method of education is so effective as the Froebelian." He adds that the games and occupations seem to meet exactly the needs of the coördinations between the senses still active and that the pupils seem to miss but little that the perfect child gains.

To no class of defectives has the kindergarten been more of a boon than to the feeble-minded. The story of those lacking in mental capacity is a sad one, and provision for their care and such development as is possible to them is still in its infancy. The present thought concerning the education of the blind and the deaf, particularly the latter, is that segregation in large institutions apart from normally constituted companions is not the best method of education. With respect to the feeble-minded, on the other hand, it is becoming more and more evident that institutional life is the only safe and sensible life. In the existing thirty-two institutions for the feeble-minded, in 1901, kindergarten instruction plays an important part. "The normal child does not need to be taught every step," says Mr. Allen again. "His powers of attention, his will, his desire, his own originality, enable him to fill the gaps in his instruction from his own daily experiences. In fact he learns more out of school than in. On the contrary the feeble-minded child has to be taught each step, hence his education is extremely slow. The simple occupations of the kindergarten fit the child of from eight to twelve years of age as they do bright children of four or five.

The teacher devises all means of busy work for them, using coarse material. No instruction is in more general use or is more helpful to the children than that of the kindergarten. After this their education continues on a very elementary plane beyond which it is impossible for them to go."

One of the most interesting developments of the decade along kindergarten lines was the introduction of the kindergarten into the government Indian schools, — the result of Professor W. N. Hailman's appointment to the superintendency of these schools in 1894. The Indian schools under governmental control are of four classes. To the first class belong the day schools, one hundred forty-three in number, in 1900. These are held in Indian villages or near encampments. They are ungraded in character, and are usually taught by a man and his wife. One of the chief purposes of these schools is to teach better modes of living as well as the rudiments of the school arts. To the second class belong the Reservation Boarding Schools, numbering seventy-five. These are graded schools partly industrial in character, maintained on the reservations. It is in these that the kindergartens have been introduced to the number of forty. Of these Professor Hailman says in Butler's "Education in the United States": "The experiment (of introducing kindergartens) proved eminently successful. The children entered into the work and games with zest and intelligence. Their traditional shyness and reticence yielded naturally and readily to their objective interest in the exercises. They acquired the English idiom with much ease and learned to express their ideas fully and with eagerness. Moreover, the use of the kindergarten methods and of kindergarten materials has entered the primary classes with similar good results. The children spend from one and one half to two hours each day in these kindergartens." In commenting upon this work in 1897, *The Kindergarten Review* said: "In the Indian schools four years ago there was not a single kindergarten. Now there are over forty, and the primary work is thoroughly vitalized with the spirit of Froebel."

To still another class — the highest — belong the Industrial Training Schools, ten in number. This list includes the school at Carlisle, Pa., which enrolls eight hundred students, Haskell Institute, at Lawrence, Kan., and several other institutions of high rank. To three of these a normal department has been added to train Indian young men and women for the work of teaching. The normal courses in these institutions correspond fairly to the courses of other normal schools. At Haskell Institute those who have completed the normal course are given the opportunity of devoting an additional year to kindergarten training under the director of the kindergartner of the institution.

Considering what has been accomplished in these different directions toward the introduction of the kindergarten into the school system, there seems no good reason for the discouragement that overzealous kindergartners occasionally feel, nor does there seem to be any immediate danger that "the kindergarten will have to go," as Polly

Oliver said of the boarders, — a prophecy sometimes expressed by its critics. Instead, according to present indications, the school system a few years hence may be voicing the sentiment expressed by a normal school president who viewed the increasing number of applicants for the kindergarten course with something like alarm, remarking, "If this keeps on, the rest of the school will soon be little more than an annex to the kindergarten department." But "new occasions bring new duties," and the twentieth century is bringing problems of its own for the twentieth-century kindergartners to solve. The reorganization of kindergarten thought and procedure that has hardly more than begun will tax the insight of the wisest before it is completed. The effect of the kindergarten upon the school and of current educational thought upon the kindergarten have not yet been clearly perceived or stated because the process is not yet completed. Superintendent C. B. Gilbert considered the introduction of the kindergarten into the public schools "the greatest step in the educational history of the country, with the exception of the founding of normal schools." But the story of the kindergarten in the school is but partially told with the recital of its introduction. The concluding chapters of the story are those that relate to its effect upon the school itself, and the reaction of the school upon its own thought and procedure. These are the topics that will be discussed in the following pages.

CHAPTER XI

KINDERGARTEN INFLUENCE IN ELEMENTARY EDUCATION

THE kindergarten has been one of the vital influences in American education. Its influence has been exerted along many different lines and upon many different groups of people. It forms a happy memory in the lives of the three million or more children who have participated in its procedure since the first kindergarten was opened in America. It has interpreted life from a higher standpoint to the twenty-five thousand or more young women who have taken courses in kindergarten training. It has aided the thousands of mothers who have made a study of its principles in meeting the daily problems of the home. It has enabled the Sunday school teachers of the land to organize the religious instruction of little children upon a more fundamental basis. It has given teachers of every grade a new insight into the educational process, and has taught them to direct the development of their pupils with more wisdom than before. That the attitude of the world toward childhood has been revolutionized during the present generation, that motherhood has taken on a new and higher significance, and that primary education has been transformed in recent years largely as a result of kindergarten influence are facts so thoroughly recognized as to need but a passing mention. In enriching the lives of the children who have participated in kindergarten procedure, in interpreting the significance of motherhood anew to the women of the land, and in setting a new and different standard for the teacher, the kindergarten has rendered an invaluable service. As the value of its influence is recognized, the extension of the kindergarten has become one of the features of educational progress.

Great as the value of the kindergarten may be to the children who participate in its exercises, its greatest service to education cannot be rendered by the mere addition of kindergartens to the graded school system. If the principles upon which kindergarten practice is based are valid, they must be valid not alone for the stage of development which the kindergarten covers but also for the other stages as well. The powers awakened during the kindergarten years need progressive and continuous exercise to reach the development of which they are capable, and unless the work that follows is based upon the same general principles the development is arrested. The fruit of the kindergarten tree needs a longer time to ripen than that afforded by the kindergarten years alone. The transformation that the work of the primary grades has undergone in recent years bears testimony to the recognition of these facts. The progress of the kindergarten movement is measured in part by the increasing number of kindergartens. It is measured no less by the increasing application of its principles to grade work. The multiplication of kindergartens is relatively a simple matter. The reorganization of the elementary school has been a task of far greater complexity. The kindergarten embodied a new ideal of education; it implied a different attitude toward childhood; it utilized for the child's development means other than the traditional ones; it employed different methods of procedure. The application of kindergarten principles to primary school practice meant nothing less, therefore, than the reorganization of the school, — the reconstruction of its ideals, the enrichment of its curriculum, the adoption of new and different methods. Since the kindergarten embodied the principles of the new educational philosophy, it alone would in great measure have effected the transformation of the school. But at the time when its influence began to be felt other forces were at work in American life — forces which created other movements destined to play a part in the transformation of American education. These movements differed in origin, aim, and scope, but all reënforced the influence exerted by the kindergarten and hastened the transformation which it would have effected. The modern primary school is the complex product of these many influences.

While the present procedure of the primary schools bears the stamp of the kindergarten too unmistakably to leave one in doubt as to the source from which the transforming influence has come, other influences have played their part and have left their impress. Of this the art and manual training movement, which next to the kindergarten has been the strongest influence in the transformation of the school, is an illustration. The child study movement and the Herbartian movement of a later date are other examples of movements that have influenced the aims and methods of elementary education and left their mark upon school work. Any discussion of kindergarten influence that does not recognize these other movements and their reciprocal influence upon the kindergarten and upon each other must therefore be inadequate. To comprehend the primary school of the present it is necessary to glance briefly at its past, and at the movements that have played a part in its transformation.

The primary school, as that term is now understood, has been in existence but little more than forty years. The system of grading that created it did not come into general use until after the Civil War. The traditional curriculum of the Three R's with which it began was gradually modified by the adoption of new subjects, and as early as the seventies it showed signs of progress. Object lessons had become general as a result of Pestalozzian influence, emanating from the Oswego Normal School. In 1870 drawing had been introduced into the schools of Boston. This was the indirect result of the London and Paris expositions in 1851 and 1867, which had shown the value of art instruction as an educational factor. Although these additions had been made in the more progressive communities, formal instruction was the rule and the repression of childish activity the established form of procedure. The word method of teaching reading had, it is true, supplanted the time-honored drill in the A, B, C's, but with few exceptions the methods of instruction had not yet been touched by the new spirit. The musical instruction, for which such books as "Loomis's First Steps" furnished the basis, was formal in the extreme, and the rote song was unrecognized. The instruction in drawing was based upon geometrical principles, and had no foundation in children's native interests. Form study did not become the basis for art instruction until 1880, and not until much later did color work become a recognized feature. The free expression of the children's ideas by means of clay modeling, paper cutting, or painting was unknown in school work. The need of physical activity in the form of play and games and the value of contact with nature were also unrecognized. The teachers having the least training and experience were placed in charge of the youngest children and paid the lowest salaries. Such was the primary school in the early seventies, when the kindergarten came.

As has been stated, the changes that have taken place in elementary education during the past thirty or more years have been the result of many different influences. These influences may be grouped into two periods, — the first beginning at about the time of the Philadelphia Exposition, and continuing until about the time of the exposition at Chicago; and the second beginning with that event and continuing until the present time. The movements exerting the greatest influence during the first of these periods were the kindergarten movement, the art and manual training movement, and the nature study movement. These movements continued their influence during the second period, but they were reënforced by the new psychology, child study, and Herbartianism. The Philadelphia Exposition was a great stimulus to art education. As a result "an immediate wave of art enthusiasm spread over the country," and art instruction became a part of the school curriculum in every progressive community. The kindergarten movement also felt the stimulus of the exposition. In 1870 there were but ten kindergartens in the United States. In 1880 the number had increased to four hundred. In spite of the fact that with the exception of those in St. Louis these kindergartens were all private or charitable, they exerted an influence upon the school system of many a city, even upon those that did not adopt them as a part of the public school system later.

The nature study movement had a different origin. The introduction of science into the colleges and universities had shown the necessity for cultivating the children's powers of observation during the early years; hence courses in nature study for the grades were advocated and attempted. The new interest in literature called also for the beginning of literary instruction in the elementary school, and hence the story began to receive recognition as an educational instrument. The influences that combined to reconstruct elementary education thus came from three different sources: from the industrial world, which demanded art instruction as a preparation for industrial life; from the colleges, which insisted that the proper intellectual habits should be formed and formed early; and from the educational reformers, who proclaimed the doctrines of Pestalozzi and Froebel as a means of awakening the people to a realization of education as something more than instruction in the traditional school arts.

Since it took time for the new influences to make themselves felt, the breaking up of the old régime did not become general until the decade between 1880 and 1890. That decade may therefore be called the decade of experiment and transition. To the uninitiated it was a decade of confusion. The addition of new subjects meant either the displacing of established ones or the overcrowding of the program, — at least a disturbing of the established order. The new subjects called also for the use of new and unfamiliar methods, — another element of uncertainty. Since teachers and even superintendents did not always understand the purposes of the new subjects, their relation to the traditional ones, and the methods to be used in presenting them, it is not strange that the results should have been unsatisfactory many times, and that discontent should have been rife, both in the teaching ranks and in the community. In course of time an adjustment to the new conditions was effected. The ideals that called for new subjects and new methods were more clearly apprehended and a new unity was worked out, both in curriculum and methods. The curriculum of the present has an organic unity of its own, based upon the experiences, the activities, and the interests of children in the different stages of development, but the school in which such a curriculum obtains is separated from the school of the eighties by an immeasurable distance. The progress made since that time is due to the kindergarten and to the movements that characterized the decade between 1890 and 1900, — the new psychology, child study, and Herbartianism. The effect of these will be touched upon later. There have been three stages, therefore, in the evolution of the modern primary school, — the first, in which the old ideals prevailed; the second, in which a transition from the old ideals and methods to the new was in progress; and the third, in which the new determine both curriculum and method. But since progress has not been equally uniform in all sections of the country, schools may be found representing each of these stages. Some still embody the old ideals and have not, therefore, progressed beyond the first stage; others, the great majority, in fact, have accepted the new ideals in theory, but are still struggling with the problems of their application; still others, relatively few in number but constantly increasing, have satisfactorily in practice worked out the new ideals.

The knowledge of educational conditions thus outlined is necessary as a background for the study of kindergarten influence and progress. It is not difficult to see how the drawing, manual training, or other movements have influenced the character and methods of the school. When the adoption of a new subject was decided upon its adaptation to the several grades was carefully considered, the teachers were given instruction in the methods to be employed, and adequate supervision was provided to meet the problems of administration. In the case of the kindergarten it was very different. When kindergartens were added to the school system, a supervisor was engaged in the larger cities, it is true, but her duties seldom included instruction to the grade teachers in the methods of applying kindergarten principles to their particular work. In fact, so little direct effort was made to bring kindergarten influence to bear upon school work that one may well ask, What means did the kindergarten adopt to affect school procedure so vitally? The introduction of drawing, music, manual training, and physical exercise into the school curriculum lessened the apparent differences between the kindergarten and the school, but did not necessarily carry with it the spirit and method of the kindergarten, nor did it insure the attitude towards childhood for which the kindergarten stands. The primary teacher of the present has absorbed the spirit of the kindergarten by observation and training, though she may be unconscious of that fact. The approval which the kindergarten received compelled the teacher of the early day, steeped in the formalism that characterized the school work of that time, to acquaint herself with kindergarten procedure, and as far as possible to adopt its spirit and method. This was no easy task. Where kindergartens existed teachers diligently visited them; when they did not exist the teachers' only resource was the available literature of the subject or attendance at some of the summer schools, such as those conducted by Colonel Parker at the Cook County Normal School, or W. N. Hailman at La Porte, Indiana, that made a specialty of the kindergarten and its principles. While the study of kindergarten theory did much to produce the change in attitude, the main source of inspiration was the kindergarten itself. The primary teacher who visited a kindergarten could not fail to be impressed by the kindergartner's attitude toward her children, — by her coöperation with them in the spirit of comradeship and by her sympathetic insight into their interests and needs. She was impressed no less by the children's attitude toward their work, by the spontaneity of their interest, and by their delight in the use of the bright-colored material. The games were a revelation to her, since they showed that there could be freedom without disorder; the interest which the children took in the kindergarten songs made her own drill on scales and intervals seem little better than drudgery; and the attractiveness of the kindergarten room gave her helpful suggestions concerning the value of beauty as a factor in education. In short, recognizing that there was possible an order of things very different from that to which she was accustomed, she determined to profit by the lesson. If kindergarten procedure could be made so interesting, why not school procedure as well? Why, she asked, should there not be pictures upon the walls and plants in the windows, in the primary room as well as in the kindergarten? Why should the kindergarten children have bright-colored material and the primary children none? Why could not the songs and many of the games used in the kindergarten be used also in the primary department? The educational leaders were beginning to ask the same questions, and to urge the utilization of childish activity in the primary grades, but no arguments were half so convincing as the example of the kindergarten itself. As a result the characteristic features of the kindergarten were to a greater or less degree adopted by the school. Exercises with kindergarten material became common, and kindergarten songs and games were incorporated into the procedure of the primary school. Since the work in drawing was not based upon form study until 1880, and color exercises formed no part of that work until many years after, the kindergarten material was a revelation to the teachers, and the gift and occupation exercises gave to many the first suggestions concerning instruction in form and color. The success of the constructive exercises carried on in the kindergarten converted many to the value and feasibility of manual training also. The expense involved in the introduction of drawing and manual training as such had delayed that introduction in many instances; but the success of the exercises of a kindergarten character, which involved but little expense, not only familiarized the teachers with the purposes and methods of these subjects, but also prepared the public for their acceptance. Where drawing and manual training had been introduced the efforts toward the adoption of kindergarten principles strengthened the work already undertaken. Where they had not, the attempts along kindergarten lines hastened such introduction. The children's interest in *doing* was in such marked contrast with their interest in mere learning — by the customary methods at least — that teachers and school boards could not fail to see that a new educational force had been discovered and a new vein of childish interest struck.

It was along such practical lines as these that the influence of the kindergarten upon the primary school was first felt. It is a question whether the so-called application of kindergarten principles to the work of the grades meant much more to the average teacher, during the decade between 1880 and 1890, than the adoption by the school of the external features of kindergarten procedure. But the mere adoption of these features led to a deeper study of Froebelian doctrine, and this in turn to an insight that resulted in better things. The fact that the kindergarten could obtain results in the line of art expression that could not be obtained by any other methods had led the advocates of art instruction as early as 1880 to reconstruct the system of art education on a basis Froebelian to the core. The result was the Prang System of Art Education. The Prang System has been one of the great agencies of educational reform and the most effective ally of the kindergarten in placing the work of the school upon an active instead of a receptive basis. Wherever the Prang System is used the principles of Froebel are disseminated. The success of the system is due in no small degree to its espousal of kindergarten principles.

It has become one of the great agencies for the spread of the kindergarten gospel.

But the art instruction was not the only line of work that was reorganized in whole or in part as a result of a growing insight into kindergarten principles. The kindergarten song book rendered an important service in carrying kindergarten influence into the school, as has been stated. Since it was the agency by means of which kindergarten games found their way into the primary schoolroom, the song book did as much as the kindergarten material to introduce the principle of activity into primary education. But acquainting primary teachers with kindergarten games was but a part of the service the song book rendered. It showed a new conception of the function of music in a child's development, and of the methods by which that development should be secured. The kindergartner maintained that this development depended upon the cultivation of musical feeling, and that this made the hearing of good music, adapted to the child's comprehension, indispensable. This practically created the child's song and brought the rote song into use as an educational instrument. She maintained further that the appreciation of rhythmic exercises and participation in them is essential, and that such exercises should therefore have a place in the kindergarten program. She further insisted that opportunity for the interpretation of music should also be given, and that there should eventually be creative expression in music, as there is such expression in other lines. But if these ideas were to obtain in the music teaching of the grades, a new system of ideals and methods was needed. The principles in question were gradually recognized, and a reorganization of the music teaching in the grades was undertaken. Such a reconstruction was hardly more than conceived of, however, during the decade in question; in fact, it has been but partially effected even yet. Because the kindergarten song book suggested such a reconstruction, and introduced games and dramatizations into the grades, it has been one of the main agencies for the spread of kindergarten influence. Wherever it has gone it has carried the kindergarten spirit — the sympathetic interpretation of childhood, the love of nature, and respect for human activity, whatever its form.

The use of the kindergarten game in the primary school led to the reorganization of another line of work also. The physical needs of school children had received but scant consideration at the hands of school authorities; but about the middle of the decade under consideration, gymnastic exercises were introduced into the schools of all the larger cities. But the spirit with which the children entered into the games, in marked contrast with the spirit manifested in the formal exercises, showed plainly that this branch of school work had not yet been placed upon a proper foundation. That there was needed a course of physical training in which games appropriate to the different grades should have a place was readily seen. Such a course was not worked out during the decade in question. Like the needed reorganization in musical lines, it is hardly worked out even yet, but much thought has been given to it in recent years.

The reorganization of the work in physical training was not the only service, however, of the kindergarten game to the primary school. The dramatic instinct, so strong in childhood, had been refused recognition along with other instincts in the school of the early days. The kindergarten recognized and utilized these instincts and this was one of the reasons for its appeal to childish interest. It gave opportunity for picture making and building, in the use of the gifts and occupations. It found occasion for the exercise of the dramatic instinct in the dramatization of human and animal activities. The dramatic game is not only an instrument of instruction peculiarly adapted to childish needs, but it is a means of expression of the greatest value. Like drawing, modeling, or building, it is a means of determining the nature of the child's mental images. The primary teacher of the early day could not fail to see the significance of dramatic and imitative play and its value for her own work, but the adoption of such play was at first impossible. To carry out dramatic games necessitated her becoming like the kindergartner, a jumping frog, a galloping horse, or a flying bird or butterfly, as occasion demanded, and from this a false dignity shrank. If the kindergartner had taught the primary teacher no other lesson than that one must become a child with the children to succeed with them, she would have rendered the school an invaluable service. The teacher had stood aloof from the children, a being apparently of a different order, and occupying a different plane. The kindergartner taught her to live with the children on their own level, yet above it. The primary teacher of the present has learned the lesson, and her success is measured by her approach to the kindergarten type. The principle of dramatic expression, introduced into the school through the avenue of the kindergarten game, has had most important results in the primary grades. It has given new life and interest to nature work; it has been the principal means by which a knowledge of the trade world has been obtained, and through the dramatization of stories it has vitalized children's interest in literature and history. Dramatic representation has demonstrated from a new standpoint what art and manual training had demonstrated from another, — that activity is the avenue to children's interest, and the surest means to their development.

In the line of nature study, too, the kindergarten has suggested new ideals and methods to the primary school. As stated elsewhere, the nature study movement in the elementary school was the indirect result of the introduction of scientific courses into the colleges and universities. The attempt to teach science to college students revealed a fundamental defect in the educational system. Students were utterly lacking in the knowledge that must form the basis for all scientific study, — the knowledge gained from direct observation. They had, moreover, no conception of scientific method, and no power of scientific reasoning. The introduction of the inductive sciences into the high schools of the country was the immediate result. The high schools, however, declared themselves unable to meet the demand this laid upon them by the higher institutions unless a foundation in the form of nature study was laid in the elementary schools. The stimulation from the higher institutions to science teaching in the grades was invaluable, but the organization of a suitable course of nature study was a difficult matter. The teachers of the period were wholly lacking in scientific knowledge, material adapted to schoolroom conditions was difficult to obtain, and the purposes of the work were but dimly perceived. The movement therefore pursued an uncertain course during the early years. The advocates of art teaching, who had encountered similar difficulties in advancing the cause of art education, had solved their difficulties by rejecting a course organized from the higher grades downward, and had constructed a new course, as has been stated, which began with the fundamental interests and capabilities of the youngest children, and proceeded upwards. The necessity for a similar reconstruction in the nature work was forced upon the friends of that movement, and it was in this direction that the kindergarten rendered valuable service.

Although the kindergarten did not solve all the difficulties of the struggling nature study movement, it exercised an appreciable influence upon the selection of subject-matter and upon the methods of work. This influence would doubtless have been more pronounced had the kindergarten in the United States been faithful

Q

to the ideals of its founder. Gardening, nature excursions, and other lines of nature work formed an organic part of the curriculum in Froebel's world-famed school at Keilhau; and every child took part in the garden work that formed a feature of the first kindergarten at Blankenburg. Miss Elizabeth Harrison said, on her return from a tour in Europe a few years ago, "Nowhere in the land of Froebel did I find a kindergarten without its little plot of ground where the children put their own seedlings, tended their own plants, plucked their own blossoms, and in the autumn gathered and stored their own multiplied seeds." Gardening for the primary grades, if not for the whole school, should have been the result of kindergarten influence and example. School gardens form an organic part of the school work in a few cities, but these are the product of the settlement or the Outdoor Art Association rather than of the kindergarten.

In spite of its failure to realize its own ideals, however, the kindergarten has contributed much that is of value along nature study lines. It has given the kindergarten children the right attitude toward nature. It has taught them to consider plants and animals as friends and helpers, having ways of their own that can only be learned by observation. It has led them to think of the domestic animals as needed helpers, deserving of care and consideration. It has given thousands of children an acquaintance with animal life by the care of pets, such as squirrels, rabbits, or doves, which can be kept in or near the kindergarten room. By means of the aquarium and terrarium it has familiarized them with the habits of fish, frogs, insects, and other lower forms. When one has come to recognize the animals of field and forest as governed by motives not unlike his own, nature can never be wholly uninteresting. The bird building its nest or feeding its young, the caterpillar spinning its cocoon, the butterfly emerging from its crysalis, the cricket chirping in the grass — these, and a thousand other things, have become significant to children during recent years.

The plant world, too, has made its appeal to the child's interest. By means of the window box, if the school garden is impossible, the children have learned of the awakening seed, the slowly forming bud and blossom, and the seed, ripening for the next year's round. The bud and blossom of springtime, the changing foliage and ripening fruit of autumn, and the snow-covered landscape of winter have been interpreted and idealized by means of song, story, and picture, until the whole realm of nature seems to the child a veritable fairyland. The kindergarten and the school have a different function to perform in the child's development, but in the nature work at least, the school has so completely adopted the aims and purposes of the kindergarten that there are no longer dividing lines. The primary school journals and the song and story books intended for use in the primary grades all reflect the spirit and method of the kindergarten in its attitude toward nature. The study of nature in the grades is successful when the emphasis is placed where the kindergarten places it — upon the care and observation of living things, upon functions rather than upon structure. The kindergarten and the art work reconstructed upon kindergarten principles have given nature study the place that it now occupies in the school curriculum and in the lives of American children.

Another line of school work that has felt the influence of the kindergarten is the story. Although the story was the first form of instruction in human history, and storytelling has occupied a place at every fireside since the world began, the story as a school instrument is a thing of the past few years, and story-telling was so rare an art among teachers that its possession was a matter of comment. The place that the story now occupies in primary work is due to two influences, that of the kindergarten, and that of Herbart and his American exponents. The Herbartians, like the advocates of nature study in an earlier period, attempted to organize a systematic course of instruction in literature for the whole school. In this the story told by the teacher was to serve as the foundation. The kindergarten began as it did in the case of nature study and drawing, from the level of the little child and worked up, leaving the grades beyond to work out their own special problems. The child had had no place in literature until the past century, and literature had made no conscious provision for the child's literary needs. The entrance to the world of fancy — the child's own by natural right — was not until recent years gained through the door of the schoolroom, and to acquaint the child with the best in literature had not been one of the recognized aims in the teaching of reading. The school which had rejected the child's desire to picture and dramatize the world about him as of value for educational purposes had failed to recognize no less the educational value of the child's love of stories. Here, too, the kindergarten took the stone which the builders had rejected and gave it an important place in the new educational edifice. The story, in the estimation of the kindergartner, is the means of interpreting to the child the life of which he is a part, and of acquainting him with the motives that actuate conduct. Since the child of kindergarten age lives in the realm of the imagination, the story that meets his needs must be clothed in the garb of fancy; since action is the first law of being during the early years, it must be dramatic; since his unfolding spiritual nature craves sustenance, it must contain seed truths to germinate and grow into right action; since his power of comprehension is limited, the story must be told instead of read.

The kindergartner's views concerning the story as an educational instrument were impressed upon the primary teachers of the early days by the successful use of the story in the kindergarten; they were spread broadcast by collections of stories by kindergartners that later found their way to the educational market. Story-telling became a feature of primary school as well as of kindergarten procedure, and the art of story-telling became one of the tests of a good primary teacher. When the Herbartian movement came somewhat later, the foundation for a course of literature for the grades was already laid. The movement to give children a knowledge of the world's best literature, resulting from the combined influence of Froebel and Herbart, has been of inestimable value to American childhood. The supplementary reader and the library as an adjunct to the schoolroom are among its results. In the use of the story, as in the use of song, nature work, or dramatic expression, the line of demarcation between the up-to-date kindergarten and the up-to-date primary department is rapidly disappearing. The kindergarten song book has been one means of bringing about the unification of the kindergarten and the school; the kindergarten story has performed a like service.

The adoption of the story as a feature of primary school work, like the adoption of the other features of kindergarten procedure, was not accomplished at once. That kindergarten influence made itself felt in the school at first along practical lines has been already stated; such influence was deepened, however, by the growing insight into the fundamental principles of the Froebelian philosophy that came with the growth of the movement. Certain positive results had been realized from kindergarten influence by the end of the decade from 1880 to 1890. The spirit and manner of the kindergartner had become the accepted standard for the primary teacher, because the attitude toward childhood for which the kindergarten stands had been accepted as the true attitude. The fundamental principle of the kindergarten — that of education through activity — had been recognized as the principle upon which primary teaching should be based, since an acquaintance with the kindergarten had shown its validity. The external features of the kindergarten — its hand work, its songs and games, its nature work and its stories, had been adopted in many schools. The method of art education had been radically reconstructed as a result of its influence, and a reconstruction of the methods of teaching music, nature study, and physical training was well under way. The decade between 1880 and 1890 was a significant one in the history of elementary education because it saw the inauguration of many new features in school work. The decade between 1890 and 1900 was even more significant, since it saw the rise of other movements destined to give more fundamental insight into the ends and means of education, and thus into the new movements themselves. To understand the later developments of the kindergarten movement and the nature of its influence upon the work of the grades, it is necessary to glance in some detail at the movements in the field of general education that characterized that decade.

CHAPTER XII

New Tendencies

The influence of the kindergarten upon the school during the decade from 1880 to 1890 had been mainly external. The form of school work had been affected but the principles underlying the changes of form were but partially grasped. The literature of the kindergarten had familiarized the public with the conception of education as a process of continuous development, a process in which the child's creative activity must play an important part. That conception was illustrated in the kindergarten itself. The adoption by the school of the features that characterized the kindergarten was an attempt to realize this conception in the grades beyond, but the teacher of insight could not fail to see that such adoption alone did not accomplish that purpose. The realization of that conception in the grades called for something much more fundamental, — the reorganization of the school work upon a new basis. Such a reorganization was begun during the last decade of the century and is still in progress. The kindergarten prepared the way for such a reorganization, but could not have effected it without the aid of the movements in general education that characterized the period, — the new psychology and child study, and in a lesser degree, Herbartianism. As a result of these movements, however, the kindergarten itself was challenged both in its theory and in its practice, and as a result has been materially modified. To understand the kindergarten situation at the present time, therefore, and the changes that are taking place in the curriculum and methods of the school, it is necessary to consider briefly the movements in question.

The doctrine of education as a process of development had been theoretically accepted long before the decade now under consideration, but that doctrine did not become effective as a reorganizing principle in school work until reënforced by other authority than that of the educational reformer. The rapid development of the biological sciences during the seventies, due to the acceptance of the theory of evolution, had given rise to a new interpretation of life. According to this interpretation both mind and body are the product of the evolutionary processes. A study of the lower forms of life, both plant and animal, had acquainted the scientist with the fundamental laws of life and growth, and the relation between the organism and its environment. The work done in these lines made a study of the mental life from the standpoint of the natural sciences necessary. The "new psychology" evolved in the universities of Germany during the seventies in response to this need, found its way to the leading institutions of America soon after. It was taught at Yale by Dr. George T. Ladd, who published the first American book of importance on physiological psychology. It was taught at Harvard by Dr. William James and at Johns Hopkins by Dr. G. Stanley Hall. Other institutions soon followed. The psychological laboratory became a part of every well-equipped educational institution, and researches in psychology were carried on by methods approved by the canons of scientific criticism. Since psychology in its new aspect emphasized the evolution of mind, the observation of children followed as a natural consequence. Genetic psychology, and in fact the whole child study movement, was therefore a logical outcome of a psychology based upon natural science methods.

The new psychology differed from the old or rational psychology in attitude, scope, emphasis, and method. Its attitude, as stated, was scientific, not philosophic. It ignored metaphysical problems such as the nature of the self and its relation to the universe, and confined itself to a study of mind as a reacting mechanism. It placed emphasis upon the study of the stream of consciousness in the process of functioning. This called for a study of the neural basis of the conscious states. The emphasis thus necessarily placed upon the study of the nervous system gave rise to the term "physiological psychology" as indicating the character of the new science. The fact that the method adopted was that which obtained in the kindred sciences of biology and physiology, — the method of observation and experiment, led to the use of the term "experimental" or "empirical." These terms failed to indicate the aim of the new psychology however, — the discovery of the laws of mental life and growth, and the principles that underlie its adjustment to environing forces. The terms in question gave little or no suggestion as to the value of the knowledge which the new psychology aimed at as a basis for a new educational structure.

The knowledge of the mental life which the new psychology demanded called for an acquaintance with the fundamental facts of child life and development, and tended in the direction of child observation and study. The impulse to child study from the genetic standpoint came from Dr. William Preyer of the University of Jena, who in 1881 published a book of notes upon the development of his own child, called "Die Seele des Kindes." Child study would doubtless have become an important phase of psychological study in the United States apart from this, however, as a result of the impulse which had brought the new psychology into existence. The child study movement of the nineties was instituted for practical rather than for theoretical reasons, however. The new psychology as such was not evolved by the educational reformer as an instrument for the reconstruction of education, although its fundamental significance for education soon became apparent. The child study movement, on the contrary, was born of the desire to find in the knowledge of the child's development at different stages, the basis for a new educational system. For the conception of education so reconstructed the world is indebted to Dr. G. Stanley Hall, who may appropriately be called the father of the child study movement. In an editorial in *The Pedagogical Seminary* in 1895, Dr. G. Stanley Hall says: "There are two ways of advancing education. The first may be subdivided into what for want of better terms we may roughly call the administrative and the logical, and the second the internal or bio-psychological. The first method works on school laws and organizations, adjustment between grades, the constitution of teachers' societies, and on the logical side draws up courses of study with due correlations, and effects reforms by working from without inwards. The second method, assuming education to be a branch of applied biology and impressed with the great difference between logical and psychological methods, gives prominence to the latter, and would work everywhere from within outwards. Our predecessors in this favored land gave us good school laws, organization and grading which we are improving as we are also buildings. Within the past year we have taken up the vast problem of revising the curriculum. Back of all these and other educational problems, however, are the nature and needs of the growing child and youth, and the best sign of the times that the present educational awakening has struck deep root and that the near future will see greater advance than the recent past, is the fact that American 'eachers are slowly realizing that the only philosophic and even rational and consistent education is ultimately based solely on a knowledge of the growth of the body, brain, and soul of the young of the human species. *The Pedagogical Seminary* finds its distinctive character and standpoint in striving to aid in the development of this genetic knowledge of childhood as the condition of all educational progress that is real or can be lasting."

The child study movement began during the decade between 1880 and 1890, but like the new psychology, did not reach its fullest development until the following one. The desire for the reconstruction of education which brought it into existence shaped the general character of the movement. Its advocates, Dr. Hall and his disciples, aimed to acquaint the public, particularly parents and teachers, with the fundamental facts of child development by means of personal observation on their part of the children with whom they came into contact, and to lead them to see the nature of an education based upon such facts. They sought to secure the coöperation of parents and teachers in collecting adequate data concerning significant aspects of child growth, and by the sifting and organizing of the data thus obtained, they hoped to obtain a body of principles upon which to base a true educational theory. Under the leadership of Dr. Hall and others, syllabi containing directions and suggestions were prepared and sent to interested individuals or to societies organized for the furthering of the movement. The topics selected for observation and study covered a wide range. The growth of the child's body at different periods as shown by weights and measurements received considerable attention. Because of the interest awakened by the new psychology in the child's native impulses and instincts, and by the motor activities in general, children's plays and games, their toys and play material, formed one of the most interesting lines of work. The drawings of children at different ages received special attention for similar reasons. The content of children's minds, their use of language, their interests and ideals, and their moral and religious conceptions at different ages — all these and many other topics were taken up for observation and study. The child study work thus carried the spirit and method of the new psychology into every intelligent home and every up-to-date schoolroom.

The interest awakened by the child study movement was nothing short of remarkable. Child study became the principal topic for discussion at teachers' meetings and educational gatherings, and the chief subject of interest in the educational journals. It was accorded a place on the program of women's clubs, and became the topic for detailed study in parents' associations, some of which were organized for the pursuit of such study. In the normal schools child study became the avenue of approach to the study of psychology and pedagogy. In the summer schools no courses were more crowded than the child study courses. In the universities child study became a recognized phase of the work in psychology. All the problems, both of the home and of the school, seemed on the way to a happy solution by its means. The wave of immediate interest in the subject has passed, but certain positive results remain. A body of facts concerning child life at different stages has been built up, and although no specific formulation of principles for the guidance of educational procedure has been made on the basis of these facts, enough has been done to produce marked effects in school work. Child study has given parents and teachers a deeper insight into the problems of education, and has brought them into sympathy with the newer movements, — the kindergarten, drawing and manual training, and nature study. It has given the average teacher a new attitude toward children, and has done much to cultivate professional interest. Many books have been written embodying in a manner more or less popular the results of the movement, and these have added to its influence. The child study movement must be considered one of the epoch-making movements in the history of American education.

The third movement to influence education in the United States during the decade between 1890 and 1900 was the Herbartian movement. The character of German pedagogy during the past quarter century has been shaped largely by the influence of Herbart, and in view of German leadership in education it is not strange that this influence should have extended to the United States. The significance of Froebel's doctrines first became apparent through their embodiment in the kindergarten. The educational theories of Herbart made their impression likewise through their application to school work. The centers of Herbartian influence in Germany are the universities of Jena, Leipzig, and Halle. The doctrines taught in the classroom by Stoy and Rein at Jena and by Ziller at Leipzig are applied in the practice schools connected with these institutions, and it is by the illustration of Herbartian principles in these schools that American educators have been converted to the Herbartian faith.

Among the exponents of the Herbartian doctrines in the United States, Dr. Charles De Garmo and Drs. Charles A. and Frank McMurry take high rank. During the early nineties these men were all connected with the Illinois Normal University at Normal, Ill., and that institution therefore became one of the principal centers from which emanated the influence of Herbart in the United States. Not only were the doctrines of Herbart taught in the classroom, but they were applied in the training school. The curriculum of the training school was reorganized on Herbartian principles as far as these were compatible with American school work, and the methods of the recitation were shaped to meet Herbartian demands. The graduates of the school were thus familiarized with Herbart's doctrines, both in theory and in practice. Probably nothing contributed more to the spread of these doctrines than the many books written by Dr. Charles A. McMurry. The first of these was "General Method," published in 1892. This is a brief general statement of the doctrines in question. "The Method of the Recitation" shows the application of these doctrines to the work of the classroom. The adoption of Herbartian methods in the schools of the country is due in no small degree to the publication of these books and the series on "Special Methods," in which the application of Herbartian principles to the different lines of school work is shown.

The study of Herbart's doctrines was materially furthered by the organization of the National Herbart Society
about the middle of the decade under consideration. This
society was auxiliary to the National Educational Association, and its members were mainly the active members
of that organization. The meetings held in connection
with those of the National Educational Association and
the Department of Superintendence attracted attention
because of the strength of their programs and the methods
of work. The papers prepared for the meetings were
printed beforehand in the form of "Year Books," and the
discussion of the papers in question formed the program.
The publications of this society contain some of the most
valuable contributions that have been made to American
educational literature, and no educational library is complete without them.

The immediate interest in the doctrines of Herbart has
waned, like the interest in child study, but the movement
as a whole has contributed much that is of value to
American education. The movement did not awaken
the interest among parents that child study awakened, it
is true, but its interest and value for the teacher cannot
be questioned. American educators have never accepted
the Herbartian doctrines in their entirety; in fact, that
acceptance has been confined mainly to certain practical
applications of his doctrines. His psychology has not
stood the test of modern scholarship; his doctrine of
apperception, however, is conceded to be one of the most
important contributions to recent pedagogical science.

R

The Culture Epoch Theory associated with Herbart's name has been rejected as the foundation for the American school curriculum; but the thought that the curriculum of the elementary school should have a character-building content has helped to give history, literature, and nature study a permanent place in grade work and made a return to the curriculum of the "Three R's" forever impossible. A school program based upon the Herbartian principle of correlation has been found impracticable; but the attempts in that direction have done much to emphasize the principle of mental economy and to make the curriculum an organic whole instead of a mere collection of unrelated subjects. The doctrine of interest needed the modification it received at the hands of American psychologists; but its discussion did much to give a more fundamental character to education. The movement in general reënforced the theory of stages in a child's development, although it considered them from a different point of view — that of the subject-matter of instruction appropriate to each. By its discussion of the essential steps in the teaching process, Herbartianism rendered a most valuable service to pedagogical science and placed classroom instruction upon a new and higher level. The doctrine of creative self-activity this movement did not recognize, and in this respect it was out of harmony with the educational theories in process of formation in American education as a result of other tendencies. In general, however, the Herbartian movement must be considered one of the most stimulating influences in American education.

The bearing of these movements upon the kindergarten, and upon the application of the principles underlying that institution to grade work, cannot yet be wholly determined. That Froebel had grasped by intuition and insight the great educational truths which psychology has in recent years been seeking to establish is admitted by all. It is not yet equally recognized, however, that the researches of recent years have thrown a flood of light upon many truths but dimly perceived or wholly unsuspected in Froebel's time. That with the advent of this larger knowledge defects would be revealed in the system of procedure which he formulated was unavoidable. The new psychology and child study brought that larger knowledge, and these movements could not fail, therefore, to affect the kindergarten, — to establish it more firmly than ever in the confidence of the people or to impair that confidence. Until the new psychology came there had been little or no criticism. During the eighties and the early nineties kindergarten procedure was considered the ideal which school practice should seek to imitate. It was not until about the middle of the decade between 1890 and 1900 that criticisms of importance began to be heard. The smallness of the kindergarten material was declared to be injurious to growing nerves and detrimental to youthful eyes. The art teacher began to question the value of the customary gift and occupation exercises as a basis for the art work of the grades, and the physical training teacher to express dissatisfaction with many of the games. All these quoted the psychologist as their authority. As the kindergarten had heretofore met with approval only, these criticisms were not easy to bear, and they occasioned the friends of the movement no little anxiety. They feared that the criticisms in question would undermine public confidence in their beloved institution and overthrow the movement which they had labored so diligently to establish. These fears not infrequently blinded them to the wholesome nature of the criticisms and to the kindly interest of the critics. They could not then see what has become apparent since, that the new psychology has been of the greatest value to the kindergarten movement, that it was needed to interpret the principles of Froebel aright even to the kindergartners themselves, and to make possible a fundamental application of those principles to grade work. The new psychology has made necessary many modifications in kindergarten procedure, and will eventually compel a reorganization of its theory. The advent of the psychologist, therefore, marked a turning point in the history of the kindergarten movement. That movement could never have attained the influence that it now exerts in the educational world, however, without the sanction of psychology and child study. For in spite of the criticism made upon certain phases of kindergarten theory and practice, the psychologist at no time posed as an opponent of the kindergarten as a whole. On the contrary he frankly recognized it as the only attempt thus far made to establish education upon a psychological basis, and commended it as an effort to realize the very ideals that he himself was seeking to establish. As a result the friends of the kindergarten were stimulated to even greater efforts in its behalf, and many who had thus far given it but little thought were led to give it favorable attention. That education is a process of development rather than a process of instruction; that play is the natural means of development during the early years; that the child's creative activity must be the main factor in his education; and that his present interests and needs rather than the demands of the future should determine the material and method to be employed, — all these principles underlying kindergarten procedure the psychologist approved, not for the kindergarten alone, but for all education.

The effect of such approval was apparent in the rapid extension of the kindergarten movement during the latter part of the decade under consideration. As stated elsewhere, in 1890 the kindergarten had secured a legal foothold in less than half a dozen states; at present kindergartens can be established at public expense in all but eleven of the states and territories of the Union. In 1890, five or six of the larger cities and twenty-five or thirty smaller ones had adopted the kindergarten as a part of the school system; in 1902 public school kindergartens were reported in four hundred forty. In 1890 not more than six of the state normal schools of the country had established kindergarten training departments; at present such departments have been organized in more than fifty. This remarkable extension cannot be attributed wholly to any one influence, it is true, but the emphasis placed by the new psychology upon kindergarten education as a type of the education that should prevail throughout the grades was a factor of no small importance.

The strengthening of the kindergarten as such in public favor reënforced the tendency toward the reorganization of primary school work on the basis of kindergarten principles. A difference in attitude toward the type of education which the kindergarten represents was clearly discernible during the years immediately following the Chicago Exposition. The evidences of kindergarten progress which the exposition afforded were so unmistakable, the approval accorded that institution by the leading educators at the Educational Congresses was so marked, and the phases of education for which it stands were seen to be so clearly in line with the most progressive tendencies that even the most skeptical could not fail to be impressed. The hesitation that still existed in the minds of some concerning the adoption of drawing, constructive work, games, and other features that had a kindergarten savor gave way to confidence in their value and enthusiasm over the results. The new movements that had been struggling for recognition and place in the school, — art instruction, manual training, games, nature work, etc., now came in with a rush, and established phases of grade work were either transformed or wholly discontinued. The drill on arithmetical tables gave way to measurement of concrete things; the learning of the parts of speech as a foundation for language training was replaced by the reproduction of stories, and the analysis of nature study material gave way to the observation and care of living plants and animals.

During the early period the kindergarten exercises, when such were introduced, served as a pleasant diversion in the customary school grind. The methods now adopted in the regular subjects made these subjects themselves interesting. All this indicated that the principles underlying the kindergarten were being grasped in their larger sense. The establishment of public playgrounds and the organization of vacation schools gave other evidence of that fact.

The changes that were gradually taking place in the curriculum and methods of the school indicated a growing comprehension of a fundamental truth proclaimed by Froebel and sanctioned by modern psychology, — that both the matter and the method employed in the different grades must originate in the children's present needs and interests instead of in the interests and needs of the future. In other words, the curriculum must be organized on a psychological basis, not as heretofore on a logical one. This is the gist of the statement so frequently misunderstood, that education at any stage is a phase of life, not a preparation for it. The work of the kindergarten is psychologically organized; the increasing tendency to organize the work of the school upon the same principle is one of the most gratifying evidences of educational progress. A few schools have grasped this principle fully and are therefore as truly Froebelian as the best kindergartens. The majority are still struggling to carry it into operation.

The reorganization of the school curriculum from the standpoint of children's present needs is one evidence of progress; the reorganization of method from the stand-point of the child's volitional interest is additional evidence. In such a reorganization, too, the kindergarten has led the way, although the new psychology has shown it with added clearness. The distinctive method of the kindergarten is the method of creative self-activity. That which has no root in the child's volition the kindergartner considers without value in his development. The fact that expression has become the keynote in primary school method shows that this principle has been accepted by the school as the foundation principle of method. In art and manual training creative self-expression along the line of the children's fundamental interests is the constant aim. In language originality in the expression of the child's own thought, whether by means of words, pictures, or dramatic action, is constantly striven for. In nature study the method pursued is one in which the child's interest and judgment play an important part. A curriculum based on children's present needs, and a method growing out of their inherent forms of activity, — these are the fundamental characteristics of kindergarten education that are being slowly but surely adopted by the schools. Dr. Monroe says: "Wherever the emphasis in school work is placed upon the activities of the child rather than upon the technique of the process of instruction, and whenever development of character and of personality is sought rather than mere importation of information and training of intellectual ability, there the Froebelian influence is to be recognized."

The influence of the kindergarten upon the school is

clearly recognizable in still another direction. That every child must be educated if social betterment is to be effected has long been conceded. But in the estimation of Froebel intellectual development as such would not alone prepare the child for the place he is to occupy in society. He maintained that the school should make the practice of the social virtues an organic part of educational procedure. The kindergarten is an illustration of this theory, and the development of the spirit of coöperation is one of the fundamental purposes in many of the kindergarten exercises. Mr. J. L. Hughes thus describes Froebel's initial effort: "Froebel's kindergarten was a little world where responsibility was shared by all, individual rights respected by all, brotherly sympathy developed by all, and voluntary coöperation practiced by all."

The use of the child's actual relation to his playmates as a means of his social development is exactly in harmony with the selection of the materials of instruction — the curriculum — from the life about him, and with the organization of method on the basis of his immediate volition. According to Froebel, education must begin on the child's level, and with the material, intellectual or social, that has already acquired a meaning to him. It must proceed by the exercise of the power or insight gained. In the social sense therefore, as well as in the intellectual, education is and must be, even from the beginning, a phase of life, not a preparation for it.

Until the kindergarten came, the school was individualistic, not social, in its tendencies. Competition between the children rather than coöperation with them was the rule. The value of coöperative effort as a means of developing the right spirit on the part of the children toward each other has been increasingly recognized in recent years. The coöperation of the members of a class, of grade with grade, or department with department for a common end is becoming an established feature in school work. Combined effort on the part of pupils has not only made possible the decoration of schoolrooms and the beautifying of school grounds, but it has brought about a different spirit among the children. Coöperative action, the principle of the kindergarten, is becoming the principle of the school. The school no less than the kindergarten is becoming a miniature society in which the laws of right conduct are learned by practice. "He that doeth shall know" is a great truth that is being increasingly recognized as the basis of educational procedure. That the curriculum must be based on the child's present needs, that method must be founded on his own self-activity, and that the social virtues must be cultivated by practice, — these principles, Froebelian in origin but sanctioned by modern psychology, are bringing about the changes in the elementary schools.

The doctrines enumerated were brought to bear upon the American school in many ways. They were impressed upon the teachers of the country with rare force and enthusiasm by Colonel Francis W. Parker, even before the decade now under consideration. Colonel Parker embodied in himself the attitude toward childhood which the new education represents, and probably did more than any other single individual in the United States to bring about the acceptance of the doctrines in question and their application to the grades. Toward the latter part of the decade from 1890 to 1900 the views enumerated received a signal reënforcement in the educational philosophy of Dr. John Dewey. That philosophy has been expressed in many books and monographs and need not be discussed here. The Herbartian movement also did much to bring about the acceptance of these views. Herbart, like Froebel, insisted upon organizing the curriculum upon the basis of the children's native interests and experiences. The effort to base the entire course of study upon the Culture Epoch theory is nothing less than an attempt to find material for instruction in the several grades, in harmony with children's fundamental interests. The correlation of studies is nothing more than an attempt to use appropriate material in accordance with the laws of mental economy. The Herbartian doctrine as such does not accept the child's creative self-activity as the underlying principle of method, but in this particular respect American educators have taken issue with those doctrines. The elementary school owes much to the Herbartian movement. The addition of literature and history to the curriculum of the grades in a form adapted to the children's comprehension is largely the result of that movement. The more fundamental insight that American teachers have gained into the principles of the teaching process, is due in part to that movement likewise. The conviction that the ultimate aim of education is ethical and social rather than intellectual has been strengthened by that influence. Herbartianism has been one of the influences in the transformation of the school. That the doctrines of Froebel interpreted, modified, and universalized by modern psychology have exercised an influence more fundamental, however, is generally recognized.

That the new psychology approved of the kindergarten in general although it objected to some aspects both of its theory and of its practice, has been elsewhere stated. With the growing incorporation of the kindergarten into the school these aspects began to attract attention. Had the kindergarten remained outside of the school system it might have remained uninfluenced by the movements that were shaping general education; its incorporation into that system made its modification inevitable. Until such incorporation became general the criticisms of the psychologist had not been brought to bear upon either kindergarten theory or practice with any force; when the school superintendent became a factor in kindergarten procedure the situation changed. From his knowledge of psychology and educational theory in the larger sense, he could point out to the kindergartner the reasons for the criticisms which the customary kindergarten procedure had called forth, and from the standpoint of official authority he could insist upon such a modification of established procedure as the new views demanded. During the latter part of the decade, therefore, the movement in the direction of kindergarten modification received a great impetus. When such modifications first began to appear, the kindergartners who had not themselves felt the pulse of the general educational movements considered them as nothing more than "a failure to understand Froebel." When the modifications became more general those advocating them were regarded as misguided individuals who had forsaken the true gods and effected an unholy alliance with the worshipers at other shrines. But as the differences between the old forms of kindergarten procedure and the new become more apparent the kindergartners of the country began to ally themselves either with those who approved of the changes in progress on the one hand or those who were opposed to them on the other. The ultimate result was the temporary division of the kindergartners of the country into conservatives and liberals, the former clinging to the established interpretation of Froebelian doctrine and the mode of procedure that Froebel is supposed to have followed, and the latter accepting the interpretation that modern psychology and child study place upon it, and modifying the procedure on the basis of that interpretation.

Although many kindergartners have not yet accepted the views for which the liberal kindergartners stand, the logic of events points to an ultimate acceptance of those views if the kindergarten is to become an organic part of the school system. The liberal kindergartner considers that psychology and child study are but elaborating the principles which Froebel himself recognized as clearly as the knowledge of his time would permit, and that the added insight of the present but furnished the means of perfecting the

institution which he did not live to complete. She therefore welcomes the light which modern science has thrown
upon the development of the child's body, even though it
may necessitate a reorganization of the games which Froebel considered adequate for its development. She recognizes the value of the idea upon which the system of
gifts and occupations is based — that of carefully organized impressions followed by adequate expression, but
psychology has taught her that much of the customary
work with both gifts and occupations requires an exact-
ness injurious to undeveloped nerves and muscles. Her
faith in creative self-activity as the fundamental article
in the kindergarten creed has not been shaken, but she
considers that much of the customary work with the
gifts and occupations is not creative in the true sense.
She accepts the Froebelian doctrine of the value of beauty
in awakening the child's higher nature, but her study of
art has shown her that the child's fundamental art interests lie along the line of representation, not along that
of formal arrangement. She yields to no one in her belief
that children may be prepared for the appreciation of
spiritual truths early, but she can accept the kindergarten doctrine of the symbol as a means to this end in its
modern interpretation only. In these and many other
respects the liberal kindergartner considers that there is
opportunity for great improvement, both in the theory
of the kindergarten and in its practice. In general she is
willing to submit both to the test of modern educational
insight, knowing that what is of true value will not be over-
thrown.

The kindergarten movement, like all other movements, has at different periods in its history needed a different service at the hands of its friends. During the period of introduction the kindergarten itself and the educational doctrines which it embodies needed to be brought to the attention of the public; at a later period legislative and other action was needed to make possible its incorporation into the school system. These two purposes have been practically accomplished. The kindergarten is well and favorably known throughout the length and breadth of the land, and kindergartens may be established at public expense in the majority of the states in the Union. A third service is needed before the kindergarten can become an organic part of the school, however, — a service that the present age and generation must render. A new interpretation of the Froebelian gospel is needed, — an interpretation which will be in harmony with current educational thought, and which will serve as the foundation for a practice free from the criticisms to which the customary practice has given rise. This need is expressed in the closing passage of Dr. John A. MacVannel's "Educational Theories of Herbart and Froebel." He says: "If Froebel's thought is to assist in the educational reconstruction as it should, it must itself be criticised and freed from certain imperfect forms in which it has become embodied. It must be modified or transformed in the light of truths brought forward by science and by the changed conditions in the Western world, — truths which it cannot afford to neglect. 'We live spiritually,' says Professor Royce, 'by outliving our formulas and thus enriching our sense of their deeper meaning.' The thought of Froebel or the thought to which the thought of Froebel has given birth must show itself capable of adaptation to the varied conditions of the novel social environment, the needs and aspirations of American life; it must be inclusive, not exclusive; it must show itself capable of reconciling its adherents within themselves, and of lifting their minds beyond the level of controversy; it must be self-assertive and yet self-critical, disowning the unquestioning attitude of the partisan. Then, and then only, can it win the triumphs for which Froebel hoped and labored, and for which his true disciples hope and labor in turn."

APPENDIX

References on Kindergarten Work in Representative
Cities

Alabama.

Alabama Notes. Kn. Rev. Vol. XIII, p. 55.
Birmingham Notes. Kn. Rev. Vol. IX, p. 397.

California.

Early Kindergarten Work in California. Kn. Mag. Vol. V,
p. 250.

The Educational Movement in California. Kn. Mag. Vol.
V, p. 30.

Notes from San Diego. Kn. Mag. Vol. V, p. 234.

The Kindergartens of Los Angeles. Kn. Mag. Vol. VI, p.
71.

Notes from Sacramento. Kn. Mag. Vol. VIII, p. 772.

Four Weeks on the Pacific Coast. Kn. Mag. Vol. X, p. 640.

Our Work in Los Angeles. Kn. Rev. Vol. VIII, p. 237.

Notes from Oakland. Kn. Rev. Vol. IX, p. 121.

The Way They do Things in Santa Barbara. Kn. Rev.
Vol. X, p. 584.

Report of the Golden Gate Kindergarten Association. Kn.
Rev. Vol. XVII, p. 569.

Colorado.

Denver Free Kindergarten Association. Kn. Mag. Vol. V,
p. 639.

Kindergarten Training in Colorado.   Kn. Mag. Vol. VIII, p. 735.

Notes on Colorado.   Kn. Mag. Vol. VIII, p. 29.

A Summer Kindergarten in Pueblo.   Kn. Rev. Vol. IX, p. 258.

Notes from Pueblo.   Kn. Rev. Vol. XI, p. 525.

Out-of-door Work in Colorado Springs.   Kn. Rev. Vol. XIV, p. 184.

Denver Notes.   Kn. Rev. Vol. IX, p. 329.

CONNECTICUT.

Four Months' Progress in Kindergarten Work.   Kn. Mag. Vol. XII, p. 396.

DISTRICT OF COLUMBIA.

The Establishment of Public School Kindergartens in Washington.   Kn. Rev. Vol. IX, p. 200.   Kn. Mag. Vol. XIV, p. 290.

Private Work Leading to the Establishment of Public Kindergartens in Washington.   Kn. Mag. Vol. XIV, p. 290.

Kindergarten Appropriation for Washington.   Kn. Mag. Vol. XII, p. 58.

The Phœbe A. Hearst Kindergarten Work in Washington. Kn. Rev. Vol. XI, p. 558.

Four Months of Progress in Kindergarten Work.   Kn. Mag. Vol. XII, p. 452.

GEORGIA.

Atlanta Notes.   Kn. Rev. Vol. IX, p. 461; Vol. XIII, p. 427; Vol. XIV, p. 60.

Eagle and Phœnix Mills Free Kindergarten. Kn. Rev. Vol. XV, p. 505.

Notes from Savannah. Kn. Rev. Vol. XII, p. 55; Vol. XIII, p. 575.

Notes from Macon. Kn. Rev. Vol. XII, p. 241.

Struggles of an Association in the Southland. Kn. Rev. Vol. XV, p. 570.

ILLINOIS.

The Evolution of the Kindergarten Idea in Chicago. Mrs. Putnam and the Froebel Association. Kn. Mag. Vol. V, p. 720.

The Chicago Free Kindergarten Association. Kn. Mag. Vol. V, p. 734.

Miss Harrison and the Chicago Kindergarten College. Kn. Mag. Vol. V, p. 729.

Kindergarten Representation at the Columbian Exposition. Kn. Mag. Vol. V, p. 402.

The Kindergarten at the Columbian Exposition. Kn. Mag. Vol. VI, p. 186.

Review of Chicago Kindergartens. Pratt Institute Monthly, November, 1895.

The Kindergarten in the Chicago Public School System, Kn. Mag. Vol. IX, p. 679.

Chicago Public Kindergartens. Kn. Rev. Vol. X, p. 568; Vol. XI, p. 485.

The Keilhau of America. Kn. Mag. Vol. X, p. 619.

Chicago Kindergarten Institute. Kn. Mag. Vol. XII, p. 573.

The Work of the Chicago Free Kindergarten Association. Kn. Mag. Vol. X, p. 509.

Kindergarten Work in the Chicago Ghetto. The Outlook, Vol. LVI, p. 212.

The Galesburg Kindergarten Normal School. Kn. Mag. Vol. XI, p. 694.

Notes from Moline. Kn. Rev. Vol. XI, p. 58.

Report from Peoria. Kn. Rev. Vol. XV, p. 448.

INDIANA.

Free Kindergarten Work in Indianapolis. Kn. Mag. Vol. XI, p. 305.

The Kindergarten Movement in Indianapolis. Kn. Mag. Vol. XII, p. 440.

The Indiana Normal Training School. Kn. Mag. Vol. XVI, p. 458.

Kindergarten Work in Indianapolis. The Century, October, 1897.

Notes from Logansport. Kn. Rev. Vol. VIII, p. 546.

Notes from Evansville. Kn. Rev. Vol. IX, p. 326.

IOWA.

Notes from Des Moines. Kn. Mag. Vol. VI, p. 577.

Regarding Iowa Kindergartens. Kn. Mag. Vol. IX, p. 531.

The Kindergarten in Des Moines. Kn. Mag. Vol. XII, p. 328.

Notes from State Normal School, Cedar Falls, Iowa. Kn. Rev. Vol. XVI, p. 126.

KANSAS.

The Central Church Kindergarten, Topeka. Kn. Rev. Vol. VIII, p. 355.

Notes from Topeka. Kn. Rev. Vol. X, p. 179.

KENTUCKY.

Louisville Free Kindergartens. Kn. Mag. Vol. I, p. 281.

A Glimpse of Louisville Kindergartens. Kn. Mag. Vol. II, p. 383.

Notes from Louisville. Kn. Mag. Vol. VI, p. 827.

Notes from Louisville. Kn. Rev. Vol. VIII, p. 444; Vol. XIII, p. 574; Vol. IX, p. 201; Vol. X, p. 176.

Four Months' Progress in Kindergarten Work. Kn. Mag. Vol. XII, p. 393.

LOUISIANA.

The Kindergarten Outlook in New Orleans. Kn. Mag. Vol. X, pp. 227, 352.

Notes from New Orleans. Kn. Rev. Vol. VII, p. 397, 445; Vol. IX, pp. 132, 398; Vol. XIII, p. 575.

MAINE.

Notes from Bangor. Kn. Mag. Vol. V, p. 310.

MARYLAND.

Four Months' Progress in Kindergarten Work. Kn. Mag. Vol. XII, p. 456.

MASSACHUSETTS.

Review of Boston Kindergartens. Pratt Institute Monthly, November 1895.

The Kindergarten in Boston. Kn. Rev. Vol. XII, p. 474.

Boston Day Nurseries. Kn. Rev. Vol. XII, p. 283.

Mornings in Boston Kindergartens. Kn. Rev. Vol. XII, pp..279, 352, 432.

Four Months' Progress in Kindergarten Work. Kn. Mag. Vol. XII, p. 454.

Winchester and its Kindergartens. Kn. Rev. Vol. XI, p. 20.
Notes from Worcester. Kn. Rev. Vol. IX, p. 655.

MICHIGAN.

Notes from Grand Rapids Kindergarten Association. Kn.
Mag. Vol. V, p. 459.

Free Kindergarten Work in Detroit. Kn. Mag. Vol. V,
p. 558; Vol. XI, p. 264.

Autumn Work in a Detroit Kindergarten. Kn. Rev. Vol.
XI, p. 83.

Sense Training in Detroit Kindergartens. Kn. Rev. Vol.
XII, pp. 186, 218, 264.

Notes from Kalamazoo. Kn. Rev. Vol. VIII, p. 195.

A Church Kindergarten. Kn. Mag. Vol. IX, p. 572.

Notes from Saginaw. Kn. Rev. Vol. XIV, p. 58.

Lucretia Willard Treat and Her Work. Kn. Mag. Vol.
XIV, p. 482.

MINNESOTA.

Reports from St. Paul. Kn. Mag. Vol. II, pp. 257, 416;
Vol. VI, p. 835.

Reports from Minneapolis. Kn. Mag. Vol. VI, p. 834.

Reports from Duluth. Kn. Mag. Vol. X, p. 297.

Four Months' Progress in Kindergarten Work. Kn. Mag.
Vol. XII, p. 459.

MISSOURI.

A Visit to St. Louis. Kn. Mag. Vol. I, p. 266.

St. Louis Froebel Society. Kn. Mag. Vol. II, p. 57.

St. Louis Kindergartens and Schools. Kn. Mag. Vol. VI,
p. 373.

A Review of St. Louis Kindergartens. Pratt Institute
Monthly, November, 1895.
Four Months' Progress in Kindergarten Work. Kansas
City. Kn. Mag. Vol. XII, p. 392.
Twenty-fifth Anniversary of St. Louis Kindergartens. Kn.
Rev. Vol. VIII, p. 675.
Notes from Kansas City. Kn. Rev. Vol. XII, p. 441; Vol.
XV, p. 578.

MONTANA.
Notes from Helena. Kn. Rev. Vol. VIII, p. 399; Vol. XIV,
p. 665.

NEBRASKA.
Notes from Lincoln. Kn. Mag. Vol. VI, p. 733.
Four Months' Progress in Kindergarten Work. Kn. Mag.
Vol. XII, p. 453.
Notes from Omaha. Kn. Rev. Vol. VIII, p. 611.

NEW HAMPSHIRE.
Four Months' Progress in Kindergarten Work. Kn. Mag.
Vol. XII, p. 459.

NEW JERSEY.
The Kindergarten in Newark. Kn. Rev. Vol. VIII, p. 292.
Notes from Morristown. Kn. Mag. Vol. VIII, p. 606.
Notes from Jersey City. Kn. Rev. Vol. VIII, p. 330.
Notes from Newark. Kn. Rev. Vol. XI, pp. 187, 316.

NEW YORK.
The Kindergarten in Rochester. Kn. Mag. Vol. V, p. 850;
Vol. XVI, p. 410. Kn. Rev. Vol. XIV, p. 841.

Brief History of the Kindergarten Movement in Jamestown. Kn. Mag. Vol. XII, p. 305.

The Kindergarten in Buffalo. Kn. Mag. Vol. V, p. 83. Kn.
Rev. Vol. IX, p. 132.

The Kindergarten in Brooklyn. Kn. Rev. Vol. X, p.
462.

Free Kindergartens in Brooklyn. Kn. Rev. Vol. XVII, p.
471.

Public School Kindergartens of Brooklyn. Kn. Rev. Vol.
XVII, p. 478.

Public Kindergartens in the Borough of Brooklyn. Kn.
Mag. Vol. XIX, p. 549.

The New York Kindergarten Association. Kn. Mag. Vol.
XI, p. 105; Vol. XVI, p. 296; Vol. XIX, p. 574. Kn.
Rev. Vol. XIV, p. 391; Vol. XVII, p. 461.

Public School Kindergarten in New York. Kn. Mag. Vol.
XI, p. 105. Kn. Rev. Vol. XV, p. 178.

Kindergarten Progress in the Public Schools of New York
City. Kn. Rev. Vol. XVII, p. 468.

History of the Kindergarten in the New York Public Schools.
Kn. Mag. Vol. XIX, p. 484.

Early Kindergarten Work in New York. Kn. Rev. Vol.
XVII, p. 458.

Settlements and Settlement Kindergartens in New York.
Kn. Mag. Vol. XIX, p. 610.

Review of New York Kindergartens. Pratt Institute
Monthly, November, 1895.

Kindergarten Department at Pratt Institute. Kn. Mag.
Vol. VIII, p. 725.

Kindergarten Training at Teachers College. Kn. Mag.
Vol. XI, p. 574.

Kindergarten Work in the Ethical Culture Schools. Kn.
Mag. Vol. XI, p. 433.
Kindergarten Training Schools in Greater New York. Kn.
Mag. Vol. XIX.
Adelphi College, p. 521.
The Elliman School, p. 538.
The Ethical Culture School, p. 511.
Teachers College, p. 532.
Kraus Seminary, p. 517.
Miss Jennie Hunter's School, p. 578.
The New York Froebel Normal, p. 540.
Pratt Institute, p. 520.
The Speyer School Experimental Playroom. Kn. Rev. Vol.
XVII, p. 137.

North Carolina.
Notes from Ashville. Kn. Mag. Vol. V, p. 234.

Ohio.
Notes from Youngstown. Kn. Mag. Vol. V, p. 151.
A Model Kindergarten Building. Kn. Mag. Vol. XV, p.
215.
Notes from Toledo. Kn. Mag. Vol. V, p. 456. Kn. Rev.
Vol. XI, p. 449.
Notes from Columbus. Kn. Mag. Vol. VIII, p. 690.
Four Months' Progress. Kn. Mag. Vol. XII, p. 398.
The Cincinnati Kindergarten Association. Kn. Mag. Vol.
XI, p. 362.
Notes from Dayton. Kn. Rev. Vol. IV, pp. 261, 656.
Notes from Cincinnati. Kn. Rev. Vol. XIII, p. 246.
Notes from Cleveland. Kn. Rev. Vol. XIII, p. 381.

OKLAHOMA.

A Kindergarten Training Course as a Department of a University. Kn. Rev. Vol. XVII, p. 51.

OREGON.

Notes from Portland. Kn. Rev. Vol. XI, p. 516.

PENNSYLVANIA.

Notes from Altoona. Kn. Mag. Vol. V, p. 850.

The Kindergarten Movement in Philadelphia. Kn. Rev. Vol. XV, p. 300.

Review of Philadelphia Kindergartens. Pratt Institute Monthly, November, 1895.

Free and Public Kindergartens of Philadelphia. Monograph by Mrs. Constance MacKenzie Durham.

Philadelphia Girls Normal School. Kn. Mag. Vol. X, p. 388.

The Kindergarten in Pennsylvania. Kn. Mag. Vol. XV, p. 489.

The Pittsburg and Allegheny Free Kindergarten Association. Kn. Mag. Vol. V, p. 717; Vol. VII, p. 593; Vol. XI, p. 421.

Work in Pittsburg. Kn. Rev. Vol. XIII, p. 455.

Growth of the Kindergarten Movement in Scranton. Kn. Rev. Vol. XIV, p. 667.

Notes from Erie. Kn. Rev. Vol. VIII, p. 331.

SOUTH CAROLINA.

Charleston and its Kindergartens. Kn. Rev. Vol. IX, p. 253.

Charleston from a Kindergarten Standpoint. Kn. Rev. Vol. X, p. 631.

Notes from Charleston.   Kn. Rev. Vol. XI, p. 57.

Notes from Rock Hill.   Kn. Rev. Vol. XI, p. 379.

SOUTH DAKOTA.

A Black Hills Kindergarten.   Kn. Mag. Vol. XIV, p. 93.

TENNESSEE.

Notes from Chattanooga.   Kn. Mag. Vol. V, p. 716.

TEXAS.

Notes from Galveston.   Kn. Mag. Vol. V, p. 376.

Notes from Fort Worth.   Kn. Rev. Vol. IX, p. 72; Vol.
XI, p. 447.

Notes from Dallas.   Kn. Rev. Vol. XIII, p. 446.

UTAH.

Kindergarten Training in the University of Utah.   Kn.
Mag. Vol. XI, p. 216.

Notes from Salt Lake City.   Kn. Rev. Vol. XI, p. 250.

VIRGINIA.

Notes from Richmond.   Kn. Rev. Vol. XII, p. 179.

Public School Kindergartens in Richmond.   Kn. Rev. Vol.
XV, p. 129.

WASHINGTON.

Notes from Tacoma.   Kn. Mag. Vol. VIII, p. 529.

Notes from Spokane.   Kn. Rev. Vol. X, p. 117.

Notes from Seattle.   Kn. Rev. Vol. XIII, p. 247.

Four Weeks in the Pacific Coast.   Kn. Mag. Vol. XI, p. 30.

WISCONSIN.

Notes from Milwaukee. Kn. Mag. Vol. V, p. 312; Vol. XI, p. 331. Kn. Rev. Vol. XV, p. 180; Vol. XVI, p. 337.

Notes from Sheboygan. Kn. Mag. Vol. V, p. 717.

Notes from Menomonie. Kn. Mag. Vol. VII, p. 552; Kn. Rev. Vol. XI, p. 315.

Notes from Wisconsin. Kn. Rev. Vol. XIII, p. 120.

The Kindergarten Movement in Wisconsin. Kn. Mag. Vol. XIV, p. 165. Kn. Rev. Vol. XVI, p. 400.

The Kindergarten Movement in Milwaukee. Kn. Mag. Vol. XVIII, p. 385.

Milwaukee a Kindergarten City. Kn. Rev. Vol. XVI, p. 387.

The Public School Kindergartens of Milwaukee. Kn. Mag. Vol. XVIII, p. 460.

Milwaukee Mission Kindergartens. Kn. Mag. Vol. XVIII, p. 462.

CANADA.

The Kindergarten in Ottawa. Kn. Mag. Vol. III, p. 150.

The Establishment and Growth of the Kindergarten in Ottawa. Kn. Rev. Vol. XVII, p. 497.

The Kindergarten in Canada. Kn. Mag. Vol. XVII, p. 325.

The Kindergarten in Canada, Toronto. Kn. Mag. Vol. XVII, p. 495.

The Kindergarten in Canada. Kn. Rev. Vol. XV, p. 463.

INDEX

[For references to cities see Appendix.]

Abbott, Jacob, 161.
Addams, Jane, 110, 111.
Adler, Felix, 18.
Æsthetic element in education, 43, 49, 50, 51, 129.
Africa, kindergartens in, 91, 92.
Alcott, Bronson, 16.
Aldrich, Mrs., 172.
Allen, Edward L., 203, 204, 205.
Allen, Louis H., 180.
American Journal of Education, see Barnard, Henry.
Anderson, Clara L., 78, 79, 176, 195, 196, 200, 202.
Andrews, E. Benjamin, 39 (quoted).
Art education: beginnings of, 5, 6, 7; stimulus of Philadelphia Exposition to, 6, 7, 38, 39, 40; introduction into elementary curriculum, 211, 212, 214, 219, 246; kindergarten influence upon, 50, 219, 220, 231, 248.
Art: in American life, 3, 39; museums, galleries, and schools, 40, 41.
Associations, *see* Kindergarten Associations.
Australasia, kindergartens in, 91.

Baker, George A., 22.
Baldwin, George J., 123.
Barnard, Henry, 14, 15, 27, 29, 159, 161–163.
Barnes, Earl, 126, 154.
Bartlett, Nellie S., 94–96.
Baum, Rosemary, 157.
Beard, Frederica, 167, 170.
Beebe, Katharine, 167.
Benefactions to kindergarten cause, 68–70.
Bigham, Madge, 178.

Biological sciences, 39, 49, 233.
Birney, Mrs. Theodore, 173.
Blake, Henry W., 180.
Blaker, Mrs. Eliza A., 66.
Blatchford, Mrs. E. W., 97.
Blind, kindergarten instruction for, 201, 203, 204.
Blow, Susan E.: and St. Louis schools, 18, 20; 16, 185 (quoted); 163, 167, 168, 171–174.
Boelte, Maria, 17, 20.
Boone, Richard G., 34 (quoted).
Bowen, H. Courthope, 167.
Bowman, Mrs. T. E., 83.
Bradley, Milton, 34, 180.
Brooks, Angeline, 135, 153.
Brown, Emerson and, 176.
Bryan, Anna E., 153.
Bureau of Education, *see* Commissioner of Education.
Burk, Frederick, 168, 172.
Burma, kindergartens in, 92.
Burritt, Ruth, 18.
Business firms, kindergartens supported by, 112, 114, 116, 117, 122, 124.
Butler, Nicholas Murray, 203, 206 (quoted).

Calkins, N. A., 161.
Cannell, Maud, 168.
Ceylon, kindergartens in, 92.
Charity, *see* Benefactions, and Philanthropy.
Chautauqua, kindergarten instruction at, 140–144.
Chenery, Susan, 177.
Cheney, Mrs. Edna D., 15.
Chicago Exposition, influence upon education of, 193, 194, 198, 246.

269

Child study movement: origin of, 235–237; spread of, 237–239; effects of, on kindergarten, 8, 243; effect on elementary education, 212–216, 246.

Children's clubs, *see* Settlements.

Children's literature, 228, 229, 230, 242, 251.

China, kindergartens in, 93.

Christian Examiner, 15, 27.

Chubb, Percival, 157.

Church: changes in doctrine of, 9, 25, 26, 43, 44, 45, 51, 52; kindergarten adoption by, 76, 77, 81; kindergartens supported by, 78, 79; value of kindergarten to, 82–85, 99; auxiliaries of, and kindergarten promotion, 79–81.

Civil War, 4, 9, 25, 39, 160.

Clarke, Isaac, 40 (quoted).

Cleveland, Mrs. Grover, 70.

Clubs, *see* Women's Clubs.

Color, use of, in art education, 213, 219, 220.

Commissioner of Education, 11, 19, 29, 58, 66, 78, 185, 194, 196; *see also* Barnard, Henry, and Harris, William T.

Compayré, Gabriel, 162.

Congress of Mothers, 59, 156.

Cooper, Mrs. Sarah B., 66–68, 77, 135, 136, 152, 154.

Corwin, Dr. Richard W., 118–122.

Crane, Rev. Caroline Bartlett, 85.

Crosby, Mary, 147.

Crouse, Mrs. J. N., 90, 154.

Current Literature, 45.

Deaf mutes, kindergarten instruction for, 201, 203.

De Garmo, Charles, 240.

Dependent children, kindergartens in homes for, 201, 202.

Dewey, John, 251.

Dexter, Edwin Grant, 144, 203, 205 (quoted).

Dickens, Charles, 27.

Dickinson, J. W., 22.

Doerflinger, Carl H., 32.

Douai, Adolph, 13, 22, 30, 36.

Dramatic expression in primary grades, 223, 224.

Du Bois, Patterson, 173.

Dwight, Fanny L., 31.

Earle, E. Lyell, 179.

Education: a college study, 49, 184, 234, 235, 238; physical, 222, 223, 231; moral, 43, 51; religious, 43, 51, 77, 86, 87, 143, 144; psychological conception of, 3–5, 9, 49, 160, 232, 233.

Educational Congresses, 147, 152–157.

Educational literature, 34, 159, 162, 182.

Educational periodicals, *see* Barnard, Henry, Hailman, W. N., Hall, G. Stanley, and Kindergarten periodicals.

Elementary school, *see* Primary school.

Emerson and Brown, 176.

Endowed kindergartens, *see* Benefactions, and Philanthropy.

England, and kindergarten movement, 6, 14, 27.

Exhibits, of kindergarten work, *see* N. E. A., I. K. U., and Expositions.

Expositions, kindergarten representation at: Philadelphia, 18; New Orleans, 147; Chicago, 148–151, 193; Atlanta, 155, 156; Omaha, 156; Buffalo, 157; St. Louis, 157, 158.

Factories, kindergartens supported by, *see* Business firms, and Welfare work.

Federation of Women's Clubs, *see* Women's Clubs.

Feeble-minded, kindergarten instruction for, 201, 205, 206.

Fisher, Laura, 19, 66, 69 (quoted).

Form study, in art education, 213, 219, 220.

Foster, Mary C., 167.

Frankenberg, Caroline Louise, 13.

Franks, Fanny, 164.

Froebel, Froebelian doctrines, Froebelian influence, 2, 4, 8, 9, 11, 14–16, 24, 26, 27, 32, 33, 36, 52, 58, 74, 163–166, 172, 185, 192, 215, 220, 230, 243, 244.

Games in primary school, 221–223.
Gardens, school, 226.
Gaynor, Mrs. Jessie L., 176.
German influence in American education, 12, 13, 14.
Gilbert, Charles B., 208.
Gilman, Mrs. Charlotte Perkins, 175.
"Goldammer's Manual," 163.
Golden Gate Kindergarten Association, see Mrs. Cooper.
Gordon, Dr., 99 (quoted).
Grabill, Mrs. Margaret, 120.
Graef, Virginia, 157.
Greene, Mrs. E. G., 105.
Gregory, Jeannette R., 167.
Grinnell, Elizabeth, 174.
Gymnastics, see Education.

Hailman, Mrs. Eudora L., 14, 22, 145, 153, 154, 176.
Hailman, William N., 13, 17, 21–23, 30–33, 36, 131, 145, 152, 154, 157, 161, 163, 166, 186, 206, 218.
Haines, Henrietta B., 17.
Hall, G. Stanley, 8, 234, 235, 237.
Hancock, John, 22.
Harding, Mary B., 93.
Harris, William T., 20–23, 34, 78, 79, 153, 186, 192, 195; see also Commissioner of Education.
Harrison, Elizabeth, 154, 166, 168, 169, 174, 177, 226.
Hart, Caroline M. C., 66, 156.
Haven, Caroline T., 136.
Hawaiian Islands, kindergartens in, 91.
Hearst, Mrs. Phœbe A., 67, 70.
Heineman, A. H., 163.
Henrotin, Mrs. Ellen M., 72.
Herbart, Herbartian movement, Herbartian influence, 212, 214, 216, 228, 229, 233, 239, 240, 241, 242, 250.
Hicks, Mary Dana, 153.
Hill, Patty S., 66, 176.
Hill, Mary D., 155, 176.

Hill, S. H., 68.
Hofer, Andrea, 179; see Mrs. Proudfoot.
Hofer, Amalie, 136, 138, 150, 156, 172, 179.
Hofer, Mari Ruef, 176, 177.
Hogan, Mrs. Louise, 173.
Holbrook, Dr. M. L., 28.
Holman, Minnie, 155.
Hopkins, Mrs. Louise Parsons, 153.
Howe, Annie L., 96–100, 153.
Howe, E. G., 153.
Howliston, Miss, 177.
Hubbard, Mrs. Clara Beeson, 176.
Hughes, Mrs. Ada Marean, 134, 135, 152.
Hughes, James L., 27, 249 (quoted), 153, 167, 171.

Idealistic philosophy, 2, 16, 25, 26, 52.
India, kindergartens in, 92, 93.
Indian schools, kindergartens in, 206, 207.
Industrial education: beginnings of manual training, 5, 6, 7; introduction of, into elementary curriculum, 38, 157, 211, 214, 216, 219, 246, 248.
International Education Series, 162, 163, 164.
International Kindergarten Union: predecessors of, 137; formation of, 134–136; growth of, 137–139; services to kindergarten cause, 139–140.
Isham, Samuel, 41 (quoted).

James, William, 8, 234.
Japan, kindergarten work in, 96–101.
Jarvis, Josephine, 31, 163, 164.
Jenks and Rust, 176.
Jenks and Walker, 176.
Johnson, Fanny L., 69.
Johnston, Bertha, 179.
Johonnot, James, 162.
Jorgenson, Ketchum and, 177.
Jourdan, Minerva, 179.
Judson, Rev. Edward, 81, 82.

Kebler, Mrs. J. A., 116.
Ketchum and Jorgenson, 177.

Kindergarten Associations: organization of, 56–58; purposes of, 56, 58; work of, 59, 61–63; results of, 59, 60, 61.

Kindergarten legislation in the different states, 187–189, 192, 193, 197–199.

Kindergarten literature: beginnings of, 27, 31, 35, 36; progress of, 159, 162–174.

Kindergarten Literature Company, 150, 179, 181.

Kindergarten periodicals: *Child Garden*, 178, 179; *Kindergarten Magazine*, 178–181; *Kindergarten Messenger*, 31–33, 36, 179; *Kindergarten News*, 180; *Kindergarten Review*, 32, 69, 178–181, 217; *New Education*, 32, 33, 166, 179.

Kindergartens in the public schools: experiment in St. Louis, 20, 21; extension of movement from 1880–1890, 184, 190, 191; from 1890 to present, 192–196.

Kindergarten training: beginnings of, 17, 20, 22; association training schools, 64, 65, 201; private training schools, 65, 200, 201; kindergarten training departments in public normal schools, 191, 192, 199, 200.

King's Daughters and kindergarten promotion, 79.

Kraus, John, 17, 22, 29, 30.

Kraus-Boelte, Mrs. Maria, 17, 22, 23, 30, 31, 36.

Kriege, Matilda, 17, 30, 35.

Krüsi, 161.

Ladd, George T., 233.

Laws, Annie, 72, 135.

Legislation, kindergarten, *see* Kindergarten legislation.

Lewis, Dr. Dio, 28.

Lindsay, Maud, 178.

Logan, Miss, 92.

Logan, Rev. Robert, 92.

Lord, Misses, 163.

McCulloch, Mary C., 135, 136, 154.

McDowell, Mary E., 106.

Mackenzie, Constance, 61–63 (quoted), 153, 154.

McMurry, Charles, 240.

McMurry, Frank, 240.

MacVannel, John A., 255 (quoted).

Mann, Horace, 16.

Mann, Mrs. Mary, 28, 30.

Mann, Mrs. Louisa, 70.

Manual training, *see* Industrial education.

Marwedel, Emma, 17, 166.

Mason, Lowell, 41.

Mathews, W. S. B., 42 (quoted).

Mexico, kindergartens in, 91.

Meyer, Bertha, 31, 36.

Meyer, Margaretha, 14, 15; *see* Mrs. Schurz.

Michaelis, Emelie, 163, 164.

Micronesia, kindergartens in, 92.

Milburn, John G., 157.

Missions, kindergartens as an agency in: in cities, 19, 23, 58, 60–63, 67, 68, 77–82; among alien peoples, 87, 90, 91; in foreign fields, 88–102.

Monroe, Paul, 248 (quoted).

Montgomery, B. E., 90.

Moore, H. Keatley, 163, 164.

Moral education, *see* Education.

Morley, Margaret, 164.

Mosher, Mrs. Martha, 173.

Mother-play book, 31, 36, 163, 164, 167; 100.

Mothers' classes, 59, 60, 142, 143, 168, 208.

Murray, May, 180.

Music: development of, in United States, 41–43; introduction into elementary curriculum, 40, 50, 213; methods of teaching, influenced by kindergarten, 50, 51, 174–177, 213, 221–222.

National Council of Women, 137.

National Educational Association: organization of, 22, 23, 130; creation of kindergarten department, 130, 131; organization of I. K. U. at Saratoga meeting of, 133–136; value to kindergarten movement of, 34, 131, 132, 137, 192.

Nature study movement: beginnings of, 214; influence of kindergarten upon, 224–228, 231, 246, 248.
Neidlinger, W. H., 176.
Newton, Frances, 156.
Newton, Rev. R. Heber, 77, 83.
Normal schools: creation of kindergarten departments in, 21, 22, 191, 192; influence upon kindergarten movement of, 65, 192, 200.

Object lessons, 160, 161.
Ogden, Mrs. Anna, 147.
Oswego Normal School, influence of, 5, 160.

Page, David, 160.
Page, Mrs. Mary B., 157.
Painting, see Art in American life.
Paris Exposition, 6, 30.
Parker, Col. Francis W., 157, 162, 186, 192, 218, 250.
Parsons, Anna Q. T., 15.
Patterson, J. H., 114–116.
Payne, Joseph, 162.
Payne, William H., 162.
Peabody, Elizabeth Palmer, 12–16, 27, 28, 31, 32, 35, 72, 137, 166.
Pestalozzi, 5, 160, 215.
Philadelphia Exposition, influence upon education of, 6, 7, 9, 18, 19, 23, 37, 41, 57, 78.
Philanthropy: increasing need of, in cities, 19, 46–48, 60, 61; organization of agencies for, 46, 47, 53, 54; the kindergarten as a philanthropic agency, 19, 23, 58, 60–63, 67, 68.
Philippines, kindergartens in, 196, 197.
Philosophy, see Idealistic philosophy.
Pierson, Clara Dillingham, 178.
Pingree, Laliah, 69, 136.
Playgrounds, establishment of, 48, 54, 110, 114, 177, 247.
Pollock, Mrs. Louise, 13, 28, 30, 35.
Pollock, Susan, 17, 31, 36, 166.
Posse, Baron Nils, 153.
Poulsson, Emelie, 32, 168, 176, 177, 180.
Poulsson, Laura, 180.
Prang system, 220, 221.

Preyer, William, 116, 235.
Primary school: the history of, 3, 4, 212, 213, 215, 216; kindergarten influence upon, 50–54, 174, 178, 186, 210, 211, 216–231.
Private kindergartens, 13, 195, 214.
Proudfoot, Mrs. Andrea Hofer, 167, 174, 179.
Psychological conception of education, see Education.
Psychology, the new, 8, 184, 214, 216, 232–235, 243–245.
Putnam, Mrs. Alice H., 18, 60, 66, 112, 154.

Ralph, Julian, 101 (quoted).
Ramabai, Pundita, 93.
Rein, William, 239.
Religion, changes in, see Church.
Religious education, see Education.
Renaissance, educational, 39.
Ronge, Bertha, 14, 28, 35.
Rousseau, 162.
Rozenkranz, 162.

Salaries of kindergartners, 126.
Saunders, Miss, 95.
Schurz, Mrs. Carl, 13–16; see also Meyer, Margaretha.
Science teaching: in colleges, 224; in secondary schools, 225; in elementary schools, 225; the new psychology a result of, 233; see also Nature study movement.
Seaver, Superintendent, 185 (quoted).
Settlements: similarity of kindergarten association to, 63, 107; methods of kindergarten akin to, 108; kindergarten as a feature in, 111, 112; value to kindergarten of adoption by, 109, 110.
Shaw, Mrs. Pauline Agassiz (Mrs. Quincy A.), 68, 69, 191.
Sheldon, E. A., 5, 160.
Sheldon, Rev. Charles E., 83–85.
Sheldon, William E., 136.
Smith, Eleanor, 101, 176.
Smith, Kate Douglas, 66.
Smith, Nora A., 67, 167–169, 174, 177.

T

Snider, Denton J., 167, 168, 172.
Social movement, the: beginnings of, 44–46, 61, 63; bearing upon education, 52–54.
Sociology, introduction into colleges, 39, 46.
Song teaching, see Music.
South America, kindergartens in, 91.
Southern Educational Association, organization of kindergarten department of, 133.
Spencer, Herbert, 23, 32.
Stanford, Mrs. Leland, 67, 71.
Steiger, E., 34, 35.
Stewart, Sarah A., 134–136, 138, 154.
Stockham, Mrs. Alice, 179.
Stockham, Cora S., 179.
Story, the: a feature in kindergarten, 174–178; adoption by primary school, 214, 228–230.
Stoy, 239.
Strong, Rev. Josiah, 45, 78 (quoted).
Summer schools, a means of propagating kindergarten doctrines, 140–146.
Sunday school, the, 77, 82, 86, 87, 143, 144, 170.
Supplementary reading, see Children's literature.
Symbolism, 254.

Temperance work, a means of kindergarten propagation, 103–107.
Theology, the new, 9; see Church.
Tomlins, William L., 152.
Treat, Mrs. Lucretia Willard, 181.
Turkey, kindergartens in, 94–96.

Vacation schools, 48, 54, 247.
Van Kirk, Mrs., 177.
Von Buelow-Wendhausen, Baroness, 139, 164.
Von Marenholz-Buelow, Baroness, 14, 27, 28, 30, 35, 164, 165.
Vreeland, Herbert, 113 (quoted).

Waldo, Eveline A., 196.
Walker, John Brisben, 173 (quoted).
Washburne, Mrs. Marion Foster, 153.
Washington, Mrs. Booker T., 73.
Welfare work, the kindergarten a feature in, 112–124.
Wheelock, Lucy, 135, 153, 163.
White, E. E., 162.
Whitmore, Eva B., 136.
Wickersham, J. P., 161.
Wiebe, Edward, 30, 35.
Wiggin, Kate Douglas, 66, 67, 166, 167, 169, 176, 177.
Wilson, Mabel, 167.
Wilson, Woodrow, 7 (quoted).
Wiltse, Sara E., 177.
Winship, A. E., 160 (quoted).
Winterburn, Mrs. Florence Hull, 173.
Wise, Margaret E., 168.
Woman's Christian Temperance Union, see Temperance.
Woman's Clubs, propagation of kindergarten movement by, 71–75.

Young Women's Christian Association, kindergartens supported by, 79.

Ziller, 239.

AMERICAN EDUCATION:
ITS MEN, IDEAS, AND INSTITUTIONS
An Arno Press/New York Times Collection

Series I

Adams, Francis. **The Free School System of the United States.** 1875.

Alcott, William A. **Confessions of a School Master.** 1839.

American Unitarian Association. **From Servitude to Service.** 1905.

Bagley, William C. **Determinism in Education.** 1925.

Barnard, Henry, editor. **Memoirs of Teachers, Educators, and Promoters and Benefactors of Education, Literature, and Science.** 1861.

Bell, Sadie. **The Church, the State, and Education in Virginia.** 1930.

Belting, Paul Everett. **The Development of the Free Public High School in Illinois to 1860.** 1919.

Berkson, Isaac B. **Theories of Americanization: A Critical Study.** 1920.

Blauch, Lloyd E. **Federal Cooperation in Agricultural Extension Work, Vocational Education, and Vocational Rehabilitation.** 1935.

Bloomfield, Meyer. **Vocational Guidance of Youth.** 1911.

Brewer, Clifton Hartwell. **A History of Religious Education in the Episcopal Church to 1835.** 1924.

Brown, Elmer Ellsworth. **The Making of Our Middle Schools.** 1902.

Brumbaugh, M. G. **Life and Works of Christopher Dock.** 1908.

Burns, Reverend J. A. **The Catholic School System in the United States.** 1908.

Burns, Reverend J. A. **The Growth and Development of the Catholic School System in the United States.** 1912.

Burton, Warren. **The District School as It Was.** 1850.

Butler, Nicholas Murray, editor. **Education in the United States.** 1900.

Butler, Vera M. **Education as Revealed By New England Newspapers prior to 1850.** 1935.

Campbell, Thomas Monroe. **The Movable School Goes to the Negro Farmer.** 1936.

Carter, James G. **Essays upon Popular Education.** 1826.

Carter, James G. **Letters to the Hon. William Prescott, LL.D., on the Free Schools of New England.** 1824.

Channing, William Ellery. **Self-Culture.** 1842.

Coe, George A. **A Social Theory of Religious Education.** 1917.

Committee on Secondary School Studies. **Report of the Committee on Secondary School Studies, Appointed at the Meeting of the National Education Association.** 1893.

Counts, George S. **Dare the School Build a New Social Order?** 1932.

Counts, George S. **The Selective Character of American Secondary Education.** 1922.

Counts, George S. **The Social Composition of Boards of Education.** 1927.

Culver, Raymond B. **Horace Mann and Religion in the Massachusetts Public Schools.** 1929.

Curoe, Philip R. V. **Educational Attitudes and Policies of Organized Labor in the United States.** 1926.

Dabney, Charles William. **Universal Education in the South.** 1936.

Dearborn, Ned Harland. **The Oswego Movement in American Education.** 1925.

De Lima, Agnes. **Our Enemy the Child.** 1926.

Dewey, John. **The Educational Situation.** 1902.

Dexter, Franklin B., editor. **Documentary History of Yale University.** 1916.

Eliot, Charles William. **Educational Reform: Essays and Addresses.** 1898.

Ensign, Forest Chester. **Compulsory School Attendance and Child Labor.** 1921.

Fitzpatrick, Edward Augustus. **The Educational Views and Influence of De Witt Clinton.** 1911.

Fleming, Sanford. **Children & Puritanism.** 1933.

Flexner, Abraham. **The American College: A Criticism.** 1908.

Foerster, Norman. **The Future of the Liberal College.** 1938.

Gilman, Daniel Coit. **University Problems in the United States.** 1898.

Hall, Samuel R. **Lectures on School-Keeping.** 1829.

Hall, Stanley G. **Adolescence: Its Psychology and Its Relations to Physiology, Anthropology, Sociology, Sex, Crime, Religion, and Education.** 1905. 2 vols.

Hansen, Allen Oscar. **Early Educational Leadership in the Ohio Valley.** 1923.

Harris, William T. **Psychologic Foundations of Education.** 1899.

Harris, William T. **Report of the Committee of Fifteen on the Elementary School.** 1895.

Harveson, Mae Elizabeth. **Catharine Esther Beecher: Pioneer Educator.** 1932.

Jackson, George Leroy. **The Development of School Support in Colonial Massachusetts.** 1909.

Kandel, I. L., editor. **Twenty-five Years of American Education.** 1924.

Kemp, William Webb. **The Support of Schools in Colonial New York by the Society for the Propagation of the Gospel in Foreign Parts.** 1913.

Kilpatrick, William Heard. **The Dutch Schools of New Netherland and Colonial New York.** 1912.

Kilpatrick, William Heard. **The Educational Frontier.** 1933.

Knight, Edgar Wallace. **The Influence of Reconstruction on Education in the South.** 1913.

Le Duc, Thomas. **Piety and Intellect at Amherst College, 1865-1912.** 1946.

Maclean, John. **History of the College of New Jersey from Its Origin in 1746 to the Commencement of 1854.** 1877.

Maddox, William Arthur. **The Free School Idea in Virginia before the Civil War.** 1918.

Mann, Horace. **Lectures on Education.** 1855.

McCadden, Joseph J. **Education in Pennsylvania, 1801-1835, and Its Debt to Roberts Vaux.** 1855.

McCallum, James Dow. **Eleazar Wheelock.** 1939.

McCuskey, Dorothy. **Bronson Alcott, Teacher.** 1940.

Meiklejohn, Alexander. **The Liberal College.** 1920.

Miller, Edward Alanson. **The History of Educational Legislation in Ohio from 1803 to 1850.** 1918.

Miller, George Frederick. **The Academy System of the State of New York.** 1922.

Monroe, Will S. **History of the Pestalozzian Movement in the United States.** 1907.

Mosely Education Commission. **Reports of the Mosely Education Commission to the United States of America October-December, 1903.** 1904.

Mowry, William A. **Recollections of a New England Educator.** 1908.

Mulhern, James. **A History of Secondary Education in Pennsylvania.** 1933.

National Herbart Society. **National Herbart Society Yearbooks 1-5, 1895-1899.** 1895-1899.

Nearing, Scott. **The New Education: A Review of Progressive Educational Movements of the Day.** 1915.

Neef, Joseph. **Sketches of a Plan and Method of Education.** 1808.

Nock, Albert Jay. **The Theory of Education in the United States.** 1932.

Norton, A. O., editor. **The First State Normal School in America: The Journals of Cyrus Pierce and Mary Swift.** 1926.

Oviatt, Edwin. **The Beginnings of Yale, 1701-1726.** 1916.

Packard, Frederic Adolphus. **The Daily Public School in the United States.** 1866.

Page, David P. **Theory and Practice of Teaching.** 1848.

Parker, Francis W. **Talks on Pedagogics: An Outline of the Theory of Concentration.** 1894.

Peabody, Elizabeth Palmer. **Record of a School.** 1835.

Porter, Noah. **The American Colleges and the American Public.** 1870.

Reigart, John Franklin. **The Lancasterian System of Instruction in the Schools of New York City.** 1916.

Reilly, Daniel F. **The School Controversy (1891-1893).** 1943.

Rice, Dr. J. M. **The Public-School System of the United States.** 1893.

Rice, Dr. J. M. **Scientific Management in Education.** 1912.

Ross, Early D. **Democracy's College: The Land-Grant Movement in the Formative Stage.** 1942.

Rugg, Harold, et al. **Curriculum-Making: Past and Present.** 1926.

Rugg, Harold, et al. **The Foundations of Curriculum-Making.** 1926.

Rugg, Harold and Shumaker, Ann. **The Child-Centered School.** 1928.

Seybolt, Robert Francis. **Apprenticeship and Apprenticeship Education in Colonial New England and New York.** 1917.

Seybolt, Robert Francis. **The Private Schools of Colonial Boston.** 1935.

Seybolt, Robert Francis. **The Public Schools of Colonial Boston.** 1935.

Sheldon, Henry D. **Student Life and Customs.** 1901.

Sherrill, Lewis Joseph. **Presbyterian Parochial Schools, 1846-1870.** 1932 .

Siljestrom, P. A. **Educational Institutions of the United States.** 1853.

Small, Walter Herbert. **Early New England Schools.** 1914.

Soltes, Mordecai. **The Yiddish Press: An Americanizing Agency.** 1925.

Stewart, George, Jr. **A History of Religious Education in Connecticut to the Middle of the Nineteenth Century.** 1924.

Storr, Richard J. **The Beginnings of Graduate Education in America.** 1953.

Stout, John Elbert. **The Development of High-School Curricula in the North Central States from 1860 to 1918.** 1921.
Suzzallo, Henry. **The Rise of Local School Supervision in Massachusetts.** 1906.
Swett, John. **Public Education in California.** 1911.
Tappan, Henry P. **University Education.** 1851.
Taylor, Howard Cromwell. **The Educational Significance of the Early Federal Land Ordinances.** 1921.
Taylor, J. Orville. **The District School.** 1834.
Tewksbury, Donald G. **The Founding of American Colleges and Universities before the Civil War.** 1932.
Thorndike, Edward L. **Educational Psychology.** 1913-1914.
True, Alfred Charles. **A History of Agricultural Education in the United States, 1785-1925.** 1929.
True, Alfred Charles. **A History of Agricultural Extension Work in the United States, 1785-1923.** 1928.
Updegraff, Harlan. **The Origin of the Moving School in Massachusetts.** 1908.
Wayland, Francis. **Thoughts on the Present Collegiate System in the United States.** 1842.
Weber, Samuel Edwin. **The Charity School Movement in Colonial Pennsylvania.** 1905.
Wells, Guy Fred. **Parish Education in Colonial Virginia.** 1923.
Wickersham, J. P. **The History of Education in Pennsylvania.** 1885.
Woodward, Calvin M. **The Manual Training School.** 1887.
Woody, Thomas. **Early Quaker Education in Pennsylvania.** 1920.
Woody, Thomas. **Quaker Education in the Colony and State of New Jersey.** 1923.
Wroth, Lawrence C. **An American Bookshelf, 1755.** 1934.

Series II

Adams, Evelyn C. **American Indian Education.** 1946.
Bailey, Joseph Cannon. **Seaman A. Knapp: Schoolmaster of American Agriculture.** 1945.
Beecher, Catharine and Harriet Beecher Stowe. **The American Woman's Home.** 1869.
Benezet, Louis T. **General Education in the Progressive College.** 1943.
Boas, Louise Schutz. **Woman's Education Begins.** 1935.
Bobbitt, Franklin. **The Curriculum.** 1918.
Bode, Boyd H. **Progressive Education at the Crossroads.** 1938.
Bourne, William Oland. **History of the Public School Society of the City of New York.** 1870.
Bronson, Walter C. **The History of Brown University, 1764-1914.** 1914.
Burstall, Sara A. **The Education of Girls in the United States.** 1894.
Butts, R. Freeman. **The College Charts Its Course.** 1939.
Caldwell, Otis W. and Stuart A. Courtis. **Then & Now in Education, 1845-1923.** 1923.
Calverton, V. F. & Samuel D. Schmalhausen, editors. **The New Generation: The Intimate Problems of Modern Parents and Children.** 1930.
Charters, W. W. **Curriculum Construction.** 1923.
Childs, John L. **Education and Morals.** 1950.

Childs, John L. Education and the Philosophy of Experimentalism. 1931.

Clapp, Elsie Ripley. Community Schools in Action. 1939.

Counts, George S. The American Road to Culture: A Social Interpretation of Education in the United States. 1930.

Counts, George S. School and Society in Chicago. 1928.

Finegan, Thomas E. Free Schools. 1921.

Fletcher, Robert Samuel. A History of Oberlin College. 1943.

Grattan, C. Hartley. In Quest of Knowledge: A Historical Perspective on Adult Education. 1955.

Hartman, Gertrude & Ann Shumaker, editors. Creative Expression. 1932.

Kandel, I. L. The Cult of Uncertainty. 1943.

Kandel, I. L. Examinations and Their Substitutes in the United States. 1936.

Kilpatrick, William Heard. Education for a Changing Civilization. 1926.

Kilpatrick, William Heard. Foundations of Method. 1925.

Kilpatrick, William Heard. The Montessori System Examined. 1914.

Lang, Ossian H., editor. Educational Creeds of the Nineteenth Century. 1898.

Learned, William S. The Quality of the Educational Process in the United States and in Europe. 1927.

Meiklejohn, Alexander. The Experimental College. 1932.

Middlekauff, Robert. Ancients and Axioms: Secondary Education in Eighteenth-Century New England. 1963.

Norwood, William Frederick. Medical Education in the United States Before the Civil War. 1944.

Parsons, Elsie W. Clews. Educational Legislation and Administration of the Colonial Governments. 1899.

Perry, Charles M. Henry Philip Tappan: Philosopher and University President. 1933.

Pierce, Bessie Louise. Civic Attitudes in American School Textbooks. 1930.

Rice, Edwin Wilbur. The Sunday-School Movement (1780-1917) and the American Sunday-School Union (1817-1917). 1917.

Robinson, James Harvey. The Humanizing of Knowledge. 1924.

Ryan, W. Carson. Studies in Early Graduate Education. 1939.

Seybolt, Robert Francis. The Evening School in Colonial America. 1925.

Seybolt, Robert Francis. Source Studies in American Colonial Education. 1925.

Todd, Lewis Paul. Wartime Relations of the Federal Government and the Public Schools, 1917-1918. 1945.

Vandewalker, Nina C. The Kindergarten in American Education. 1908.

Ward, Florence Elizabeth. The Montessori Method and the American School. 1913.

West, Andrew Fleming. Short Papers on American Liberal Education. 1907.

Wright, Marion M. Thompson. The Education of Negroes in New Jersey. 1941.

Supplement

The Social Frontier (Frontiers of Democracy). Vols. 1-10, 1934-1943.